TIME
ANNUAL
2004

By the Editors of TIME

TIME
ANNUAL

2004
By the Editors of TIME

28

The Year in Review

Nation

War in Iraq

Person of the Year

World

Business

122

CONTENTS

Society

136

Anniversaries

Sport

Science

146

The Arts

Milestones

158

Cover credits: Clarence S. Bull—MPTV; Brooks Kraft—Corbis;
Chris Hondros—Getty Images; Bettmann Corbis; Christian Keenan—
Getty Images; Stephan Savoia—AP/Wide World; Filippo Monteforte—
EPA/Wide World; Mirrorpix—Getty Images; Sandy Huffaker—
Getty Images; Dr. Scott Lieberman—AP/Wide World.
Back cover, clockwise from top left: Alex Livesey—Getty Images;
NASA; Robert Giroux—Getty Images

TIME ANNUAL 2004

EDITOR	Kelly Knauer
DESIGNER	Ellen Fanning
PICTURE EDITOR	Patricia Cadley
RESEARCH DIRECTOR/WRITER	Matthew McCann Fenton
PRODUCTION EDITOR	Michael Skinner
COPY EDITOR	Bruce Christopher Carr

TIME INC. HOME ENTERTAINMENT

PRESIDENT	Rob Gursha
VICE PRESIDENT, BRANDED BUSINESSES	David Arfine
VICE PRESIDENT, NEW PRODUCT DEVELOPMENT	Richard Fraiman
EXECUTIVE DIRECTOR, MARKETING SERVICES	Carol Pittard
DIRECTOR, RETAIL & SPECIAL SALES	Tom Mifsud
DIRECTOR OF FINANCE	Tricia Griffin
ASSISTANT MARKETING DIRECTOR	Ann Marie Doherty
PREPRESS MANAGER	Emily Rabin
BOOK PRODUCTION MANAGER	Jonathan Polsky
MARKETING MANAGER	Sarah Stumpf

SPECIAL THANKS TO:

Bozena Bannett, Alex Bliss, Bernadette Corbie, Robert Dente, Gina Di Meglio, Anne-Michelle Gallero, Peter Harper, Suzanne Janso, Robert Marasco, Natalie McCrea, Mary Jane Rigoroso, Steven Sandonato, Grace Sullivan

THE WORK OF THE FOLLOWING *TIME* STAFF MEMBERS AND CONTRIBUTORS IS FEATURED IN THIS VOLUME:

Kathleen Adams, Melissa August, Perry Bacon Jr., Harriet Barovick, Hannah Beech, Brian Bennett, Lisa Beyer, Laura Bradford, Timothy J. Burger, Massimo Calabresi, James Carney, Jeff Chu, Howard Chua-Eoan, John Cloud, Adam Cohen, Wendy Cole, Matthew Cooper, Richard Corliss, Simon Crittle, Bruce Crumley, Lisa Takeuchi Cullen, Pat Dawson, Jeanne DeQuine, John F. Dickerson, Sally B. Donnelly, Andrea Dorfman, Michael Duffy, Daniel Eisenberg, Simon Elegant, Michael Elliott, Philip Elmer-DeWitt, Steven Erlanger, Stephan Faris, Christopher John Farley, Matthew Forney, Stefanie Friedhoff, Nancy Gibbs, Helen Gibson, Frederic Golden, Andrew Goldstein, Christine Gorman, James Graff, Peter Hawthorne, Paul Gray, Karl Taro Greenfeld, Sean Gregory, Lev Grossman, Anita Hamilton, Ghulam Hasnain, Syed Talat Hassain, Rita Healy, John Heilemann, Marc Hequet, Avery Holton, Susan Jakes, Daniel Kadlec, Naeemah Khabir, Barbara Kiviat, Jeffrey Kluger, Joshua Kucera, Richard Lacayo, John Larkin, Michael D. Lemonick, Belinda Luscombe, Jessica Lynch, Donald Macintyre, Malcolm Macpherson, Scott Macleod, Rian Malan, J.F.O. McAllister, Terry McCarthy, Johanna McGeary, Tim McGirk, Marguerite Michaels, Siobhan Morrissey, Jodie Morse, J. Madeleine Nash, Michele Orecklin, Peta Owens-Liston, Tim Padgett, Priscilla Painton, Alice Park, Andrew Perrin, Alex Perry, James Poniewozik, Eric Pooley, Andrew Purvis, Paul Quinn-Judge, Josh Quittner, Romesh Ratnesar, Jessica Reaves, Matt Rees, Amanda Ripley, Simon Robinson, Daffyd Roderick, Wilson Rothman, Nir Rosen, Eric Roston, Andrea Sachs, Richard Schickel, Elaine Shannon, Nelly Sindayen, Joel Stein, Richard Stengel, Sonja Steptoe, Ron Stodghill II, Stewart Stogel, Chris Taylor, Jason Tedjasukmana, Cathy Booth Thomas, Mark Thompson, Jyoti Thottam, Karen Tumulty, Josh Tyrangiel, Jill Underwood, David Van Biema, Vivienne Wait, Douglas C. Waller, Claudia Wallis, Michael Ware, Cindy Waxer, Michael Weisskopf, Leigh Anne Williams, Huang Yong, Kim Yooseung, Adam Zagorin, Richard Zoglin

SPECIAL THANKS TO:

Ken Baierlein, Barbara Dudley Davis, John Dragonetti, Richard Duncan, Ed Gabel, Arthur Hochstein, Edward L. Jamieson, Kevin Kelly, Joe Lertola, Michele Stephenson, Lamarr Tsufura, Lon Tweeten, Cornelis Verwaal, Miriam Winocour

2003: LOOKING BACK

The attacks of Sept. 11, 2001, gave Americans a new motto—United We Stand. Two years later, the response to the strikes divided us. When President Bush led the U.S. into a war with Iraq, many Americans questioned his strategy, and some major allies shunned the coalition. Yet the saddest divisions were personal, not political, as soldiers— like U.S. Navy Hospital Corpsman John Lonika— hugged their families and headed for a far-off front.

Photograph by Stephen Morton—Getty Images

■ **April 9**

Sic Semper Tyrannis

In an act of iconoclasm broadcast live around the world, a statue of Saddam Hussein is brought down in Baghdad's Paradise Square, ending the 8,000-day reign of the Iraqi strongman. The symbolic take-down occurred only 21 days after the first American bombs dropped on Iraq's capital, commencing the second U.S.-led invasion of Saddam's nation in 12 years. The chain at left is attached to a U.S. tank-recovery vehicle; Lieut. Colonel Bryan P. McCoy of the 3/4 Battalion of the 7th Marines ordered the statue brought down, an act of enormous significance in Muslim culture, where such images carry special power.

■ **May 1**

Top Gun's Victory Lap

After clambering out of *Navy One*, an S-3B Viking jet, George W. Bush makes his way through cheering crew members on the flight deck of the aircraft carrier U.S.S. *Abraham Lincoln*. The President landed to deliver a prime-time address to the nation in which he declared the U.S. had accomplished its mission in Iraq. No one could deny that the White House had crafted one of the most dramatic photo-ops in memory. But such staged events have a way of slipping their surly bonds: the photo became a litmus test for Americans' view of the war and the President. Bush's admirers saw a take-charge tough guy; his detractors saw a preening pretender crowing over an incomplete victory. Administration foes assailed the cost of the event and pointed out that the carrier was so close to American soil it had to be ordered to slow down for the fly-in, while TV cameras were carefully positioned to avoid showing the San Diego skyline in the background.

June 2 ■

Bagged and Tagged

Soldiers from the U.S. Army's 82nd Airborne Division guard an Afghan prisoner in the nation's eastern section. With the attention of the U.S. government and military focused on the war in Iraq, the forces of the deposed Taliban regrouped in Afghanistan and Pakistan in the summer and showed they were back in business by launching a a series of raids and bombings that claimed scores of lives. Pro-U.S. Afghans claimed that the "neo-Taliban" is guided by many of the same men who ran Afghanistan's theocracy from 1996 through 2001. Taliban Commander of the Faithful Mullah Mohammed Omar remains at large.

Photograph by Darren McCollester—Getty Images

Photograph for **TIME** by Brooks Kraft—Corbis

■ **January 29**

Seeking Guidance

President George W. Bush, who came to religion later in his life, opens every meeting of his Cabinet with a prayer. This photograph, taken on the morning of the President's State of the Union address, captures one of the major pressure points of his Administration: the President prays for guidance while seated between Secretary of State Colin Powell and Secretary of Defense Donald Rumsfeld. The two antagonists—one a proponent of cautious multilateral diplomacy, the other an advocate for an aggressive, unilateral foreign policy— battled through the year to influence Bush's agenda.

■October 27

Line of Fire

In the Golden State, fall
is the time of maximum
wildfire danger. That's when
hot, dry winds—the infamous
Santa Anas—barrel out of the
desert, driving small blazes to
savage frenzy. And that's just
what happened on Oct. 21,
when the first of a series of
horrific blazes struck
Southern California, raging
east of San Diego and north
and east of Los Angeles. One
major fire was sparked by a
lost hunter who lit a "small"
fire as a rescue signal; it soon
got out of hand. Some 14,000
fire fighters battled to halt the
flames, which some called
one of the worst natural
disasters in California history.
The infernos enveloped more
than 750,000 acres, killed 20
people and destroyed nearly
3,000 houses. Here they
threaten homes in the Scripps
Ranch suburb of San Diego.

February 1 ■

Out of Its Element

It came from outer space, bearing wonder—and sorrow. Neighbors gathered to gawk at the strange orb that fell from the sky and landed in the yard of Marlin Hughes, a Nacogdoches, Texas, chicken farmer. The metal sphere was detritus from the space shuttle *Columbia*, which broke into pieces as it re-entered Earth's atmosphere some 207,000 ft. (40 miles) over west Texas at 8:59 a.m. The tragedy claimed the lives of seven astronauts and left a debris trail across 500 square miles of Texas and Louisiana. Several people were arrested for pilfering remnants of the craft, a federal offense.

■ **August 15**

Going My Way?

Manhattanites are happy to grab a lift after the largest power failure in history turned off the lights and snarled mass transit in New York City, Cleveland, Detroit, Toronto and other cities of the East Coast, the upper Midwest and Canada. The smiles here tell the story: though the blackout occurred at the height of an August heat wave, most city dwellers weathered the crisis with good humor and civility—in stark contrast to the bad old days of 1977, when a blackout led to widespread looting in the streets of New York City. This time around, a police car cruising by a Tribeca bar turned on the bullhorn to advise patrons, "Attention! Make sure you drink your beer before it gets warm."

Photograph by Guang Niu—Reuters—Landov

■ **May 16**

Love Is in the Air

And that's not all. With China's health officials struggling to contain an outbreak of SARS (severe acute respiratory syndrome), New Yorker Mathieu Borysevicz plays it safe as he busses his bride, Zhang Yu of Beijing, at their wedding-photo session in Tiananmen Square. Chinese authorities succeeded in hushing up the initial outbreak of the disease in the fall of 2002. But by March 2003, the potentially fatal disease had afflicted thousands of people in China and had spread to Hong Kong and Canada. Strong measures kept a lid on the epidemic, but the economies of tourist-friendly Hong Kong and Toronto languished when the cities were placed under quarantine.

Images

September 7 ■

No More
Mr. Someday

Appearances to the contrary, Andy Roddick isn't preparing to launch his head across the net: he's simply expressing his shock at winning America's premier tennis tournament, the U.S. Open. Dominating Spain's Juan Carlos Ferrero in straight sets, Roddick achieved two milestones. Only a week after turning 21, he snagged his first major title, following years of being touted as the game's Next Big Thing. And he became the first U.S. male player to show superstar potential since the salad days of Andre Agassi and Pete Sampras. Boasting such magnetic players as Serena and Venus Williams, Jennifer Capriati and Kim Clijsters, the women's game has outpaced the men's in popularity in recent years. Roddick's triumph served notice that a new generation of men were ready to battle for the fans' respect.

S C R A P B O O K

IN THE SPOTLIGHT

History may be a portrait gallery of great lives, but it's also a curio case of passing snapshots: people worth remembering, even if their minutes of fame don't quite add up to 15

Mohammed Saeed al-Sahhaf
Minister of Information, Iraq

He wasn't TIME's Man of the Year 2003, but al-Sahhaf, a.k.a. "Baghdad Bob," won the nod as America's Favorite Enemy Propagandist. Lying with the insouciance of a bass fisherman with a few bourbons in him, the Minister of Disinformation denied that U.S. G.I.s had taken the Baghdad airport, calling images to the contrary a "Hollywood trick." The day before the capital fell, he denied that "infidel Americans" were even in the vicinity. Small wonder the website WeLoveTheIraqiInformationMinister.com was deluged with as many as 4,000 visitors a second. "He's my man," said First Fan George W. Bush.

Tony Blair
Prime Minister of Britain

When President George W. Bush went looking for allies to join his "coalition of the willing" against Saddam Hussein, one man quickly raised his hand: Tony Blair. The British PM, 50, went out on a limb with his support for Bush; antiwar sentiment ran deep in Britain. In 2002 Blair's government issued a white paper that accused Saddam of hiding weapons of mass destruction. But in July 2003 David Kelly, a bioweapons analyst who had told the BBC that Blair's government had "sexed up" the report, killed himself. Blair's six-year hold on power was imperiled, but his opponents were also in disarray; the Tories canned leader Iain Duncan-Smith in October.

J.M. Coetzee
Author

The only writer ever to win Britain's prestigious Booker Prize twice didn't show up for either ceremony, so the Nobel Committee shouldn't have been surprised when they couldn't track down John Maxwell Coetzee to inform him privately that he had won the 2003 Nobel Prize for Literature before making the news public.

The reclusive genius, whom the committee described as a "scrupulous doubter, ruthless in his criticism of the cruel rationalism and cosmetic morality of Western civilization," is a native South African who writes in understated, clinically precise terms about the moral anguish and horrifying violence that result when race, culture and politics collide. Although Coetzee's best novels—*Dusklands, Waiting for the Barbarians, Life & Times of Michael K, Disgrace*—are often set in South Africa, they transform local dilemmas into universal parables. This son of a sheep farmer returns often to his signature theme: the redemptive power of adversity and humiliation.

Shirin Ebadi
Lawyer, Activist

Nobel Peace Prize winner Ebadi claimed she had no idea she was a candidate for the award. But the first Iranian and first Muslim woman to be so honored shouldn't have been shocked. Since Iran's 1979 revolution, Ebadi, 56, has been a quiet but tenacious advocate for the rights of Iranians persecuted by the hard-line regime. Along the way, she has earned a reputation for being not so much radical as militantly reasonable. "There is absolutely nothing incompatible or contradictory about Islam, democracy and political freedom," she argues.

Paul Wolfowitz
Deputy Secretary of Defense

On Sept. 15, 2001—four days after the historic terrorist attacks on America—Paul Wolfowitz advised George Bush not to wage war against Afghanistan but to invade Iraq and depose Saddam Hussein. Wolfowitz lost that battle but not the war. He spent the following months laying out the case for taking out Saddam, and the Bush team finally bought them, cementing Wolfowitz's reputation as Washington's top hawk and the Administration's most influential strategist. Since 1973, when he left his teaching job at Yale to join the Nixon Administration, Wolfowitz, 59, has served under every President except Clinton. Along the way, the onetime mathematician has won powerful patrons—including Donald Rumsfeld, his current boss, and Dick Cheney, for whom he worked during the first Bush Administration. Wolfowitz, who had steadily argued for the U.S. to remove Saddam since the conclusion of the first Gulf War in 1991, got a taste of his own war up close in October, when the hotel in which he was staying in Baghdad was hit by missile fire. Wolfowitz escaped injury.

Michael Bloomberg
Mayor of New York City

Rudolph Giuliani is a tough act to follow. TIME's Man of the Year 2001 remains widely respected for the grace and grit with which he braved the disaster that befell New York City on Sept. 11, 2001, when he was mayor. But in August, his successor, billionaire Michael Bloomberg, demonstrated that he could also keep his cool when crisis struck. Shortly after his city was blacked out by a power failure, Bloomberg appeared in shirtsleeves before microphones to assure citizens that terrorism was not involved and to urge them to remain calm. He asked New Yorkers to take the following day off, treating it as a snow day—a charming image with the mercury in the 90s. "There are worse things than taking a summer Friday off from work," he declared. His city skated through the outage.

Bloomberg, 61, earned his billions on Wall Street, where it pays to keep calm amid chaos. His term as mayor has been rough, for he has had to deal with the severe financial fallout resulting from 9/11. His remedy, a tough-love regimen of cost cuts and tax hikes, succeeded in keeping the city's budget on an even keel, but his popularity took a deep dive as a result. Posterity—and New Yorkers—may rate him higher someday.

Rush Limbaugh
Conservative Commentator

To his legions of "dittoheads," Rush Limbaugh, 52, seems to have a ready answer to all the world's ills. But Rush's bluster lost its luster in 2003. First, he resigned under fire from his role as commentator for ESPN after he claimed that Philadelphia Eagles quarterback Donovan McNabb had been hyped by the media simply because he was black. Only days later, Limbaugh—always a hard-liner on drug abuse—told his radio audience that he was addicted to painkillers and would immediately enter a rehab facility to kick the habit.

Al Franken
Liberal Humorist

He's come a long way from his role as Stuart Smalley, *Saturday Night Live's* smarmy sultan of self-help. Franken led a posse of liberal critics who published books deriding George Bush and the G.O.P. right in 2003. When Franken displayed Fox TV analyst Bill O'Reilly on the cover of his spoofing book *Lies and the Lying Liars Who Tell Them: A Fair and Balanced Look at the Right*, O'Reilly urged Fox to sue; the judge quickly threw out the suit. The publicity put Franken's rant atop the best-seller lists, with Al laughing all the way.

SCRAPBOOK

Natalie Maines
Musician

The music world thrives on stereotypes: all rappers are nasty, all divas are ditzy, all rockers are rebels, few punks are hunks, and all country singers are patriotic. Scratch that last one: at a London concert just before Gulf War II began, Texan Natalie Maines, 29, lead singer of country superstars the Dixie Chicks, declared, "Just so you know, we're ashamed the President of the United States is from Texas." The backlash was swift: country stations banned Chicks songs; fans trashed their CDs; the Rev. Jerry Falwell fulminated. Maines apologized—sort of. Within weeks, the Chicks had more to say, appearing nude on the cover of ENTERTAINMENT WEEKLY, with terms including traitor, boycott and Dixie Sluts scrawled on their flesh.

Johnny Depp
Actor

Hollywood was bewildered: Johnny Depp (*Edward Scissorhands*), known to love working for auteurs like Tim Burton and John Waters, was teaming up with Gore Verbinski, director of the Budweiser frog ads, on … a pirate movie? Surprise: Depp's hilariously overdone turn as Captain Jack Sparrow—based on Rolling Stone Keith Richards—helped turn *Pirates of the Caribbean* into a summer smash. Depp, 40, also made waves with his indelible portrayal of a rogue CIA agent in Robert Rodriguez's *Once Upon a Time in Mexico*—and with his remarks questioning the U.S. invasion of Iraq.

Felix Baumgartner
Daredevil

Don't try this at home: on July 31, the Austrian stuntman (or madman, take your pick) jumped from a plane at 30,000 ft. With a 6-ft., carbon-fiber wing strapped to his back and a supply of oxygen handy, Baumgartner glided 22 miles to Calais, France, reaching speeds of 217 m.p.h. Of his 14-min. jaunt, the 34-year-old former auto mechanic remarked, "It's very cold up there." How to train for the feat? Baumgartner's regimen included wild rides strapped atop a speeding Porsche (to accustom himself to high wind speeds), as well as practice leaps from the statue of Christ in Rio de Janeiro.

Jerry Bruckheimer
Film and Television Producer

Many of Hollywood's best moviemakers have tried to create television shows. The vast majority have failed—but they're not Jerry Bruckheimer. The most successful producer in film history, with $12.5 billion in worldwide box-office receipts from such movies as *Top Gun*, *Armageddon* and *Con Air*, he is on his way to becoming one of the most successful producers in the history of TV. He's one of the few to have three shows hit the Top 10 simultaneously: CBS's *CSI*, *CSI: Miami* and *Without a Trace*.

Surprisingly, Bruckheimer, 57, has managed this feat with shockingly few of the over-the-top effects he likes to deploy in his movies: exploding Hummers, exploding choppers, exploding cigarette boats—and, well, whatever else blows up real good. Bruckheimer's secret? He makes TV that looks better and moves faster than the usual network fare. "I just want to keep the story moving," he told TIME. "I try to take the air out, just like in our movies." All three of his shows start at Point A and end, completely resolved an hour later, at Point B. Another secret: Bruckheimer brings to TV the sleek, big-budget look of his films. His directors, set designers, costumers and even makeup artists work in the movies. Which brings us back to the film world, where the producer scored another monster success in 2003. His *Pirates of the Caribbean* was not only a surprise summer smash, but it also revived the most dormant of movie genres, the pirate flick. One word, Jerry: *Aaaargghh!*

Roy Horn
Animal Trainer

He is widely regarded by his peers in the circus world as one of the greatest animal trainers. Yet Roy Horn—one half, with magician Siegfried Fischbacher, of the famed Las Vegas performing duo Siegfried and Roy—was perhaps even better known as the target of cheap jokes. The duo, partners of 45 years, were lampooned on *Saturday Night Live* as flaming gay stereotypes. They were the poster boys (not without cause) for ultra-tacky Las Vegas performance excess.

But on Oct. 4, when Horn, 59, was attacked by one of his signature white tigers, the insults stopped. Horn had been performing with the

cat, Montecore, in the duo's $110-a-ticket show at the Mirage Hotel, when the 600-lb. beast tore at his throat and dragged him offstage, severely wounded. Some in the audience thought it was part of the act; it wasn't. Horn survived —after a struggle—but the show shut down, idling hundreds of workers. Horn's halting words as he waited for the ambulance to arrive: "Don't shoot [the tiger]."

Aron Ralston
Mountaineer

Aron Ralston, a 27-year-old outdoorsman, was reported missing on May 1 when he didn't show up for work at a mountaineering store in Aspen, Colo. Five days before, Ralston had been rock climbing alone in a Utah canyon, 40 miles from the nearest paved road and on a trail rarely used by others, when a boulder crashed down on his right arm, pinning him in a 3-ft.-wide space. Ralston fought hard, but the rock wouldn't budge. By Day 3 his water had run out. As Day 5 dawned, he was badly dehydrated and knew he must free himself by any means. So he reached for his pocketknife and began cutting off his arm,

severing it below the elbow. Then he fashioned a tourniquet to stanch the blood, used his remaining arm to rappel 50 to 75 ft. to the canyon floor and hiked seven miles to find help. Weak and bleeding profusely, Ralston linked up with two other hikers; law officers spotted the group from a helicopter. Once aboard, the gutsy climber had a single request: water.

Yao Ming
Professional Basketball Player

Surprise! The National Basketball Association's best shot at filling the shoes of the retiring Michael Jordan arrived with a familiar stamp: Made in China. Yao Ming is his name; 7 ft. 5 in. is his frame; mighty is his game. Next stop: fame. For Yao, 23, is a charmer. The Houston Rockets center loves Starbucks, computer games and SUVs, and when his Great Wall of a face cracks a smile, arenas light up. NBA fans chose Yao over the Lakers' Shaquille O'Neal as the Western Conference's starting center in the 2003 All-Star Game. Yao also surpassed Shaq in the eyes of blue-chip companies like Apple and Visa. Marketers see him as the pitchman messiah who might open the wallets of China's 1.3 billion consumers, for whom Mao was then, but Yao is now.

Bethany Hamilton
Surfer Girl

At 13, the native of Hawaii's Kauai Island is one of the best amateur surfers in the world. On Nov. 3, she was floating 1,000 yds. offshore when a shark surfaced and tore off her left arm below the shoulder. A friend's father towed her ashore, made a tourniquet from his rubber board leash and stopped the bleeding. Hamilton recovered quickly and vowed to ride the waves again.

DID I SAY THAT?

We're afraid you did—and we can prove it. Herein, a year's worth of quick quips, sizzling sound bites, good laughs and verbal gaffes

NABIL MOUNZER—EPA/WIDE WORLD

❝You're thinking of Europe as Germany and France. I don't. I think that's old Europe.**❞**
—DONALD RUMSFELD, Defense Secretary, in response to a question about European efforts to slow down the U.S. march against Iraq

❝At my age, old is a term of endearment.**❞**
—RUMSFELD, speaking to reporters the following day, after his remarks caused a furor in Germany and France

❝This isn't even trickle-down economics. It's mist-down economics.**❞**
—KEVIN PHILLIPS, political commentator, reacting to Bush's plan to eliminate taxes on stock dividends

❝I'm sure I'll end up there. Or I'll shrink my head and put it in a glass box in the living room.**❞**
—LISA MARIE PRESLEY, on whether she plans to be interred at Graceland after her death

❝My vision is to make the most diverse state on earth, and we have people from every planet on the earth in this state.**❞**
—GRAY DAVIS, California Governor, at a press conference

❝Sitting around in a big base camp and knocking back cans of beer—I don't particularly regard as mountaineering.**❞**
—SIR EDMUND HILLARY, Mount Everest pioneer, on the upsurge in amateur climbers since his 1953 climb

JENNIFER GRAYLOCK—AP/WIDE WORLD

❝Sundance is weird. The movies are weird—you actually have to think about them when you watch them.**❞**
—BRITNEY SPEARS, pop singer, at the Sundance Film Festival

❝I really do believe that we will be greeted as liberators.**❞**
—DICK CHENEY, Vice President, on his expectations for the impending Iraq war

❝You see that flag, Mr. Reid? That's the flag of the United States of America. That flag will fly there long after this is all fogotten.**❞**
—WILLIAM YOUNG, federal district judge, sentencing shoe bomber Richard Reid to life in prison

❝I am allergic to alcohol and narcotics. I break out in handcuffs.**❞**
—ROBERT DOWNEY JR., actor and substance abuser

❝I'm 49, but I never lived a single day. Only now will I start living.**❞**
—YUSSUF ABED KAZIM, Baghdad imam who used a sledgehammer to help topple a statue of Saddam Hussein

❝I studied that pot in graduate school.**❞**
—LIEUT. COLONEL MATTHEW BOGDANOS, U.S. Marine Corps Reserve officer, examining a clay pot recovered after looting in Iraq

JAMES DEVANEY—WIREIMAGE.COM

❝He thought I was some kind of airhead academic, and I thought he was rather an arrogant young member of Congress. Probably we were both right.**❞**
—DICK CHENEY, at an awards ceremony, recalling his first meeting with Secretary of Defense Donald Rumsfeld, in 1968

❝Roses are red/ Violets are blue/ Oh my, lump in the bed/ How I've missed you.**❞**
—GEORGE W. BUSH, in a poem written to his wife upon her return from a trip abroad, as read by Laura Bush at the opening of the National Book Festival

LAWRENCE JACKSON—AP/WIDE WORLD

BOB ROSS—CHICKEN OF THE SEA

"Is this chicken what I have, or is this fish? I know it's tuna, but it says 'chicken by the sea.'"
—JESSICA SIMPSON, pop singer, to her husband Nick Lachey on MTV's reality show *Newlyweds: Nick & Jessica*

"Lies run sprints, but the truth runs marathons."
—MICHAEL JACKSON, after being charged with child molestation

JOHN MABANGLO—EPA/WIDE WORLD

"We're ashamed the President of the United States is from Texas."
—NATALIE MAINES, lead singer of the Texan country trio Dixie Chicks, at a concert in London weeks before the Iraq war began

"There's an old Texas expression: If you don't have anything nice to say, go to London and say it in front of 20,000 people."
—MAINES, some months older and wiser

"He should be so lucky."
—ANDREA MITCHELL, NBC correspondent and wife of Federal Reserve Chairman Alan Greenspan, on a typo in ABC's *World News Tonight's* closed captioning that said Greenspan was recovering from surgery for an "enlarged prostitute"

"I'm going to tell all. Whoo-ee, there are going to be a lot of nervous people around here."
—TRENT LOTT, Republican Senator from Mississippi, who was ousted as majority leader, about the book he's thinking of writing

"I actually woke up and smelled the coffee."
—CHRISTOPHER REEVE, actor, after regaining his sense of smell when doctors put electrodes in his chest that helped him breathe

LUKE PALMISANO—AP/WIDE WORLD

"The battle that we're in is a spiritual battle. Satan wants to destroy this nation, he wants to destroy us as a nation, and he wants to destroy us as a Christian army."
—LIEUT. GENERAL WILLIAM BOYKIN, new Deputy Under Secretary of Defense for Intelligence, characterizing the war on terrorism as a religious battle

HALL OF SHAME

"From a business perspective, it's great for the NBA."
—MARK CUBAN, owner of the Dallas Mavericks, on Kobe Bryant's sexual-assault case

"I play fairly high stakes. I adhere to the law. I don't play the 'milk money.' I don't put my family at risk, and I don't owe anyone anything."
—BILL BENNETT, conservative activist, on his being a high-stakes casino gambler who lost millions of dollars over the past decade

"I expect a great reward in heaven. I am looking forward to glory."
—PAUL HILL, former minister convicted of killing an abortion doctor and his escort, on the eve of his execution

"I fooled some of the most brilliant people in journalism."
—JAYSON BLAIR, former New York *Times* reporter, who resigned from the newspaper after the discovery of many fabrications in stories he had written

"I hope she misses the cut. Why? Because she doesn't belong out here."
—VIJAY SINGH, golf pro, on Annika Sorenstam's playing in the Colonial tournament; he later apologized and she professed no ill will

"Now the children will not leave the house. They just sit at home all day watching satellite TV."
—LAMIA YOUNIS, mother of four, on electric power being restored with greater reliability and frequency across Iraq

"Is the United Nations on a different planet? Are reports from here totally unread south of the Hudson?"
—HANS BLIX, retiring chief U.N. weapons inspector, asking why the U.S. expected to find prohibited weapons in Iraq when his team had reported none prior to the war

"I'm like a little baby left at a doorstep, needing a woman to take care of me. Maybe I'll just have to date for the rest of my life. Or maybe the love of my life is yet to come."
—TED TURNER, on his attempt to find a new life after stepping down as vice chairman of AOL Time Warner and losing billions of dollars when the company's stock plunged

ERIK S. LESSER—EPA/WIDE WORLD

Gone with The Wind

May is the cruelest month across the broad swath of America's midsection known as the Tornado Belt. In 2003, deadly twisters born of giant supercell storms struck portions of eight states on Sunday, May 4, killing 41 people in widely scattered locations, from the devastated Kansas City, Kans., suburb above to the hilltop towns of western Tennessee.

Nation

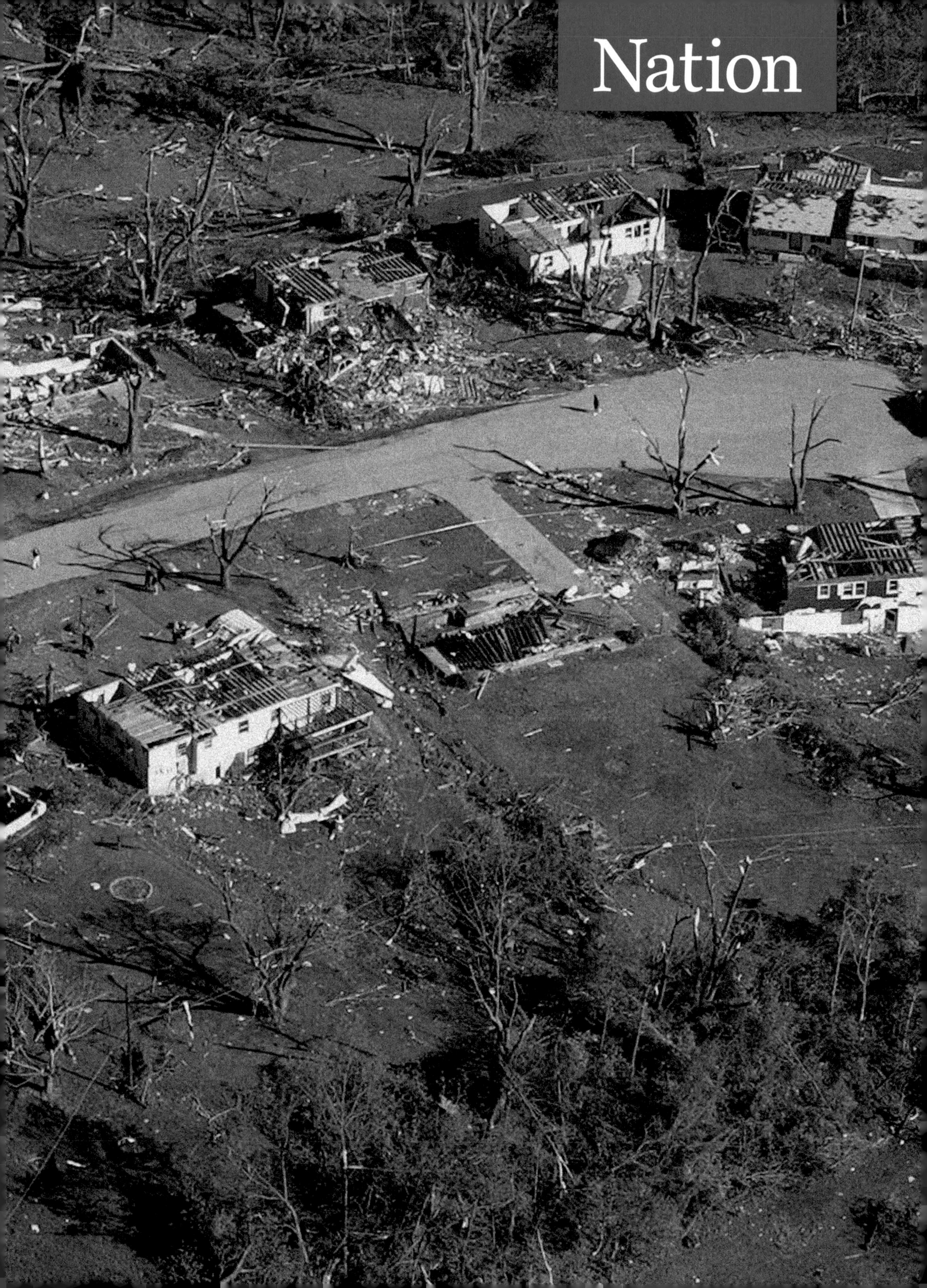

ICONS: Schwarzenegger and wife Maria Shriver unite two strands of American royalty, the Kennedy family and Hollywood stardom

RECALLED, TOTALLY

Action hero turned politician, Arnold Schwarzenegger sweeps
Governor Gray Davis out of office in a recall election in California

WHO SAYS ARNOLD SCHWARZENEGGER DOESN'T DE-serve an Oscar for acting? On Aug. 6, as he prepared to step onto the *Tonight Show* stage, host Jay Leno asked the Austrian-born action hero if he had changed his mind on his decision not to run for Governor of California in the upcoming recall election. "I am bowing out," the star murmured. And that's what everyone was expecting to hear. But a few minutes later, the former Mr. Universe declared to a squealing studio audience, "I am going to run for Governor of the state of California."

As a political debut, it was dazzling stagecraft. But even before Schwarzenegger was introduced into the equation with his rallying cry to "clean house in Sacramento," California's Oct. 7 vote on whether to remove Gray Davis from the Governor's office was shaping up to be the most surreal spectacle in U.S. politics since the 2000 Florida recount. Arnold's entry kicked the carnival up a notch; in

an off-year for national elections, the California recall story became must-see politics, a reality show for the cable news channels. Conan the Candidate joined a horse race of 135 nags—including socialite turned populist cable pundit Arianna Huffington, former baseball commissioner Peter Ueberroth, *Hustler* boss and free-speech advocate Larry Flynt and porn star Mary Carey. There were even some politicians on the ballot, including Davis' fellow Democrat and the state's lieutenant governor, Cruz Bustamante, and a well-known conservative Republican state senator, Tom McClintock. The prize: a budget mess to clean up and 34 million famously ungovernable Californians to lead.

Davis' chances of surviving weren't looking so great before Schwarzenegger entered the race—even though he had not been charged with malfeasance in office. With Californians blaming him for the epic budget problems that had brought a tripling of vehicle-license fees, a 30%

OUT: Governor Davis, with wife Sharon at his side, concedes his defeat on the evening of the vote

The recall story became must-see politics, a reality show for the cable-news channels ■

hike in state college fees and cutbacks in health services, polls showed 50% of voters supported recall when the actor entered the race. Weeks before, California's Democratic House members had privately decided among themselves that Davis was history; they pleaded with Senator Dianne Feinstein, the most popular politician in the state, to join the race. Feinstein took a pass. After Arnold's announcement, so did G.O.P. Congressman Darrel Issa, the force behind the recall movement, who had spent $2.96 million to get the proposition (and himself) on the ballot.

In the weeks that followed, Schwarzenegger ran a campaign notable for its nonengagement; he ducked debates, ducked questions and ducked labels. After all, what do you call an advocate of fiscal discipline whose one major political act had been to sponsor a successful 2002 ballot measure that required California to spend more than $400 million on after-school programs? What do you call a Republican who was pro-choice; strongly supported gay rights, including adoption rights; and favored gun control? What do you call someone who claims to be an environmentalist but has done more than any other single American to popularize the gas-guzzling Hummer?

And did we mention this rising Republican is married to a Kennedy? In fact, his turnaround on the race may have come when his wife Maria—daughter of John F. Kennedy's sister Eunice Shriver and Peace Corps founder Sargent Shriver—overcame initial hesitation about his candidacy.

Arnold's manifest contradictions may be an outgrowth of his two formative experiences: an iron-heel upbringing in Austria followed by a steady rise to fame and success in America. Schwarzenegger was born in Thal, Austria; his father was a policeman—and a Nazi. But though the actor was strongly criticized for inviting former U.N. chief Kurt Waldheim, also an ex-Nazi, to his lavish 1986 wedding to

Shriver, in typical fashion Arnold defused charges of anti-Semitism by going on to raise millions for the Simon Wiesenthal Center in Los Angeles and its Museum of Tolerance.

But it was the latter part of his life that would haunt the candidate in the days to come. Everyone knew that the star had come to America as a 21-year-old, determined to make his mark in the bodybuilding world. But few recalled the interview he gave to *Oui* magazine in 1977, in which he openly discussed smoking marijuana and participating in group sex. However moldy, the interview raised eyebrows when it was fed to the media. But worse was to come. On Oct. 2, the Los Angeles *Times* reported that six different women had come forward to accuse the actor of sexual harassment. The stories included embarrassing allegations: one woman said the star had groped her breast; another claimed he had cornered and fondled her in an elevator. More women made similar charges in the days that followed.

Schwarzenegger took a hit, but his opponents couldn't seem to get traction—and the voters' urgent desire for change swept away any doubts about the star's questionable past, relations with women and imprecise positions on the issues. On Oct. 7, Arnold was propelled into office, winning 49% of the vote in what was the largest turnout for a gubernatorial election in more than 20 years. Davis conceded—graciously—and Arnold soon traveled to Washington to meet with the President and congressional leaders. As he was inaugurated as Governor on Nov. 17, there

IN: Schwarzenegger went to Washington to meet with the President and legislative leaders after he was elected

Schwarzenegger, a moderate, ducked debates, ducked questions and ducked labels ■

was no question that the movie star had pulled off one of the most remarkable political debuts of recent decades.

For Arnold, pumped up by fame, the election may have been the easy part of his journey. The hard part—solving the Golden State's mountain of fiscal woes—lay ahead. Neither celebrity nor the Kennedy mystique nor movie mojo would seem to be of service in that quest. But if this Austrian bodybuilder with a funny Mitteleuropean accent can became a box-office king in America and then Governor of California, what exactly can't he do? ■

BOB GRAHAM

DICK GEPHARDT

JOE LIEBERMAN

JOHN KERRY

JOHN EDWARDS

WESLEY CLA

BOB GRAHAM
AGE: 67
FUNDS: $5 MILLION

The moderate from Florida, a 17-year Senate veteran, was popular with his peers but didn't catch on with voters. On Oct. 7, he was first to withdraw from the contest. Weeks later, he said he would retire from his Senate seat

RICHARD GEPHARDT
AGE: 62
FUNDS: $14 MILLION

The former House minority leader, from St. Louis, Mo., enjoyed his usual strong support from labor but lost a few major union endorsements to Howard Dean. Gephardt was expected to be a strong contender

JOSEPH LIEBERMAN
AGE: 61
FUNDS: $12 MILLION

Al Gore's 2000 running mate was the most centrist of the group. He supported the war in Iraq but criticized Bush's tax cuts. He enjoyed good name recognition, and though his fund raising lagged early, it soon bounced back

JOHN KERRY
AGE: 59
FUNDS: $20 MILLION

The Massachusetts Senator, a decorated Vietnam veteran, was touted as an early favorite, but after the insurgents Howard Dean and Wesley Clark drained some of the vitality from his campaign, he fired some key staffers

JOHN EDWARDS
AGE: 50
FUNDS: $15 MILLION

The Senator from North Carolina liked to portray himself as the candidate of the common man and stressed his humble origins (omitting the millions he made in the law). The moderate hoped to do well with Southern voters

AT THE STARTING LINE

HOWARD DEAN

AL SHARPTON

CAROL MOSELEY BRAUN

DENNIS KUCINICH

First there were 10—and here they are: the Democratic contenders who set out to win the party's nomination to face George Bush in the 2004 election. One said he'd drop out, and then there were nine ...

Y OU CAN'T TELL THE PLAYERS WITHOUT A SCORECARD. And you needed one to keep track of the Democrats vying for the party's nomination to challenge George W. Bush for the presidency in 2004. The picture above, taken Sept. 25, 2003, was made obsolete when Senator Bob Graham withdrew on Oct. 7. It will no doubt be even more out of date by the time this book reaches print. But for the record, these were the nine men and one woman who were the contestants in the long race to the nomination when the field was largest, including former general Wesley Clark , who entered the contest on Sept. 16.

The state of play, as of mid-December 2003? Presumed front runners John Kerry, Dick Gephardt and John Edwards had been rocked by the strong showing of former Vermont Governor Howard Dean, who raised $14 million in three months on the Web. The entry of Clark further rattled the pack. The two biggest surprises were Al Gore's endorsement of Dean on Dec. 9 and the capture of Saddam Hussein four days later, a victory for George W. Bush that made the road to the Oval Office look even more daunting. ∎

WESLEY CLARK
AGE: 58
FUNDS: $3.5 MILLION

The ex-general who commanded NATO troops in Europe hit the ground running when he entered the race in September. The Arkansan was a strong critic of Bush on Iraq; some said he was a stalking horse for Hillary Clinton

HOWARD DEAN
AGE: 55
FUNDS: $25 MILLION

The physician shot to the head of the pack early with a new-look, Web-based campaign that won over younger voters. Al Gore's backing was huge—but party elders worried that Dean was too hot-headed and too far left to beat Bush

AL SHARPTON
AGE: 49
FUNDS: $258,729

The Brooklyn clergyman, a longtime and divisive figure in New York City politics, won attention with his zingy one-liners. Though few believed he'd be the nominee, his run helped him put the Tawana Brawley episode behind him

CAROL MOSELEY BRAUN
AGE: 56
FUNDS: $342,519

The former Illinois Senator seemed to most to be a long shot to win the race. She pitched her platform directly to women voters, with an emphasis on child care, health care and abortion rights

DENNIS KUCINICH
AGE: 57
FUNDS: $3 MILLION

Terming himself a progressive, the longtime Ohio politician, now in the House, was perhaps the farthest left of the candidates. A strong critic of NAFTA, he also called for the U.S. to withdraw from the WTO

Campaign funds raised through 3rd quarter, 2003. Source: Federal Election Commission

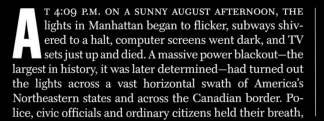

AT 4:09 P.M. ON A SUNNY AUGUST AFTERNOON, THE lights in Manhattan began to flicker, subways shivered to a halt, computer screens went dark, and TV sets just up and died. A massive power blackout—the largest in history, it was later determined—had turned out the lights across a vast horizontal swath of America's Northeastern states and across the Canadian border. Police, civic officials and ordinary citizens held their breath, recalling the scars of past blackouts that turned into grim free-for-alls of looting and despair.

And then—nothing happened. Instead of exploding, the cities fell quiet. Horns didn't honk. Although there were nasty exceptions here and there, most shopkeepers didn't gouge, and windows didn't shatter, and most of the fires were coming off grills. Peaceful Ottawa saw more looting than Detroit or Toledo, Ohio. For Americans still spooked

LIGHTS OUT!

A massive power outage leaves New York City,
Toronto, Detroit and Cleveland in the dark
but illuminates the new civility of big cities

**THE MATRIX: Auto headlights trace glittering
necklaces across Manhattan, darkened on Aug. 15
by the largest power failure in North American history**

by terrorist attacks, this latest test of people's nerve and
grace found them equipped with both. In Toronto deli and
store owners sold bottles of water for less than the usual
price; people shared cabs in the city and cell phones at the
airport. In Ohio the Akron *Beacon Journal* printed a special
edition of its rival, the Cleveland *Plain Dealer*, whose editors typed up reporters' notes by flashlight. In Harlem a
group of women in large hats outside a small Pentecostal

church set up a table with cups and plastic pitchers of iced
tea and lemonade; they were giving drinks away.

Some blacked-out regions, like Connecticut, regained
power on the night of the event, but it would be three or
even four days in some cities—notably Detroit—before the
juice was flowing in every neighborhood.

Why didn't people panic? Perhaps because word went
out quickly from every public official from President Bush

1 Electricity starts at the **power plant,** produced by a spinning **generator** driven by various means: a hydroelectric dam, a large diesel engine, a gas turbine or a steam turbine. The steam is created by burning coal, oil or natural gas or by a nuclear reactor

2 At a **transmission substation,** large transformers increase the voltage from thousands to hundreds of thousands of volts so the power can be shipped long distances

3 The electricity travels along **high-voltage lines** to a **power substation.** There, the power can be redirected to other high-power lines or stepped down to a lower voltage that is sent to neighborhood power lines

4 Power grids are a delicate balance between supply and demand in which sudden fluctuations can cause portions to fail. If, for example, a transmission line breaks, the system is designed to isolate the problem and disconnect it from the grid

6

5

1 Power plant

Generator

2 Transmission substation

TROUBLE ALL DOWN THE LINE

In just a few minutes, a glitch in the Midwest rippled through about 100 electric plants, plunging millions into darkness

A Wired World

North America is crisscrossed by thousands of power-transmission lines linking generators and cities in a complex web designed to send power where it is needed

The Lake Erie Loop

Investigators now think the crisis started with the failure of several transmission lines near Lake Erie. The clockwise flow of power around the lake was very suddenly sucked backward, destabilizing the flow of electricity

MICH.   CANADA

Toronto

Detroit   Lake Erie

Cleveland   N.Y.

OHIO   PA.

WIS.

Lake Michigan   MICH.   Lake Huron

C A N A D A
ONT.   Ottawa

Toronto   Lake Ontario

ILL.   Detroit   Lake Erie

IND.   Cleveland

OHIO

PA.

N.Y.   VT.   N.H.   MAINE

MASS.

CONN.

R.I.

New York City

MD.

KY.   W.VA.   VA.   N.J.   DEL.

*Size of circle indicates relative generating capacity of plant. Powerline data ©Platts POWERmap & Cartography

POWER-PLANT TYPE

● Coal, oil or gas
○ Nuclear
● Hydroelectric

■ States and provinces affected by the blackout

— Major transmission line

▲ Substations

CAN SPREAD

In the 2003 case, control mechanisms—computers, circuit breakers and switches—failed to contain the problem quickly, causing rapid fluctuations at substations elsewhere in the grid, tripping more shutdown mechanisms

6 The problem spread fast back to generating plants that then were producing too much or too little electricity, causing more shutdowns. Eventually, the problem was contained, preventing a blackout that could have spread as widely as the entire eastern half of the U.S.

High-voltage transmission lines

Power substation

Power substation

POWERFUL NUMBERS
The biggest blackout in North American history set all sorts of records

50 million people in the U.S. and Canada affected

8 states and **2** Canadian provinces experienced power failures

3 deaths attributed to the blackout

22 U.S. and Canadian nuclear plants shut down

10 major airports shut down

700 flights canceled nationwide

850 arrests on the night of the blackout in New York City (compared with 950 on a typical night)

23 cases of looting reported in Ottawa

7,600 gal. (29,000 liters) of drinking water distributed by the National Guard in Cleveland after the city's four main pumping stations failed

350,000 people on the New York City subway when the power went out. Nineteen trains were in underwater tunnels

Sources: North American Electric Reliability Council; Department of Energy; ESRI; AP; Philadelphia *Inquirer*; New York *Times*; How Stuff Works

TIME Graphic by Ed Gabel and Jackson Dykman; text by Missy Adams

on down that there was no evidence of any kind of terrorist attack. There was no sign of a bomb or a break-in at a utility, nor that the outage might have been a more subtle, cyberterrorist assault.

Although officials were quick to say what hadn't happened, they were initially at a loss to explain precisely what had, even though the underlying cause of the problem was all too obvious. Over the past 10 years, electricity demand has jumped 30%, but transmission capacity has increased only half that much. Electricity, which used to be consumed near its point of creation, is now routinely sold as a commodity and moved across a vast, interconnected grid—a grid never designed to move high voltage for long distances. Because everything is tied together, too much strain in one place can cause the whole system to snap.

For years now, energy experts have been warning that the grid was antiquated and inadequate. But a combination of market forces, political foot dragging and the reluctance of people to welcome high-voltage lines or towers in their backyards has made it almost impossible to create a transmission system that can keep up with demand.

In early November, a joint U.S.-Canadian task force released a preliminary report on the causes of the blackout. It found that no single cause led to the outage, but that it had resulted from a string of coincidences, each of which exploited a different vulnerability in the electrical grid that serves both nations. A key weakness that officials declared they would rectify is the voluntary, self-regulating nature of the rules governing the power grid. By autumn, both Washington and Ottawa were considering an overhaul to set mandatory, system-wide standards for all companies that generate, transmit or distribute power, complete with strict government enforcement powers. The details would not be finalized until 2004, but universal rules and accountability would be firsts.

Meanwhile, half a world away on that dark August day, the few residents of U.S.-occupied Baghdad lucky enough to have electricity sat transfixed in front of their television sets, watching the citizens of the superpower grope about in the dark. "We stayed up for an hour watching it," said one taxi driver, "until the electricity shut down." ∎

SEPTEMBER ELEGIES

Finalists are chosen in the contest to design a memorial at New York
City's World Trade Center to honor the victims of the 9/11 attacks

HOW BEST TO HONOR THE VICTIMS OF THE 9/11 ATTACKS on New York City's World Trade Center? Here are the finalists in an international contest to design a memorial feature within the overall site plan by German architect Daniel Libeskind that was approved in 2002. From 5,201 submissions, 8 finalists were chosen by a 13-member jury representing the Lower Manhattan Development Corporation. Each proposal meets certain criteria: preserving the footprints of the Twin Towers—that is, the space they occupied on the ground; listing the name of each victim; reserving a private area for families of the deceased and to hold unidentified remains. Some criticized the designs for failing to include any artifact of the tragedy itself: none of the finalists chose to display harsh reminders of the day's horrors; instead, they favored a palette of soothing effects—falling water, beams of light and gardens. ∎

VOTIVES IN SUSPENSION · Norman Lee and Michael Lewis
In "dual sanctuary spaces" under the towers' footprints,
votive lights hang from the ceiling—one per victim—over
a reflecting pool. Names are etched on exterior walls

THE MEMORIAL CLOUD· bbc art + architecture
A "cloud" of 10,000 vertical-light pathways floats above a
floor on which every victim's name is engraved in a circle of
light. Rescuers are honored in a separate grouping of names

LOWER WATERS • Bradley Campbell and Matthias Neumann
A memorial building in the north tower's footprint features a rectangular waterfall dropping into a pool, while a wall of names lists each victim. A grove of trees occupies the footprint of the south tower, and an underground Museum of September 11 revisits the day of the attacks and allows visitors to see the bedrock on the site

DUAL MEMORY• Brian Strawn and Karla Sierralta
Portals in the north tower's footprint, one for each victim, channel beams of light into a belowground gallery featuring shifting images and accounts of the victims. Aboveground, a stand of 92 sugar maple trees is enclosed by a stone wall bearing "messages of hope" from countries around the world

REFLECTING ABSENCE • Michael Arad
Each tower footprint contains a pool 30 ft. below street level, fed by water cascading down the sides. Here, the victims' names are etched on the walls. A hall connecting the sunken pools offers candles for visitors to light

SUSPENDING MEMORY • Joseph Karadin with Hsin-Yi Wu
Glass columns, one for each victim of the attacks, are placed amid trees in a pair of gardens planted in the footprints of the towers. Each victim is also recalled in a square protruding from a stone wall, while water trickling over the squares enters a "pool of tears." A water feature with a connecting bridge recalls the 9/11 events in Pennsylvania and Washington

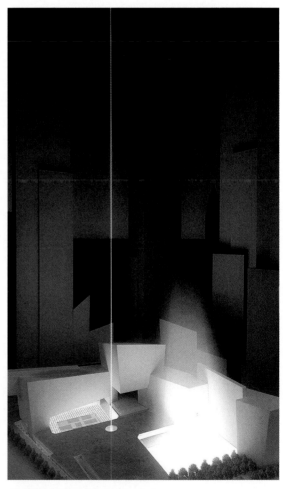

INVERSION OF LIGHT • Toshio Sasaki
The floor plan of the north tower is illuminated from below, while the south tower's footprint is a reflecting pool above a circle of lights; between them, a laser beam shines into the sky. Belowground, the names of the victims fill a glass wall, with water flowing down it

■ PROFILE

Accused Snipers in Court

The fall of 2003 saw trials begin for both suspects in the 2002 series of Washington-area shootings that left 10 people dead, three wounded and the region terrified. The trial of John Allen Muhammad, 42, started first, on Oct. 14. Though Muhammad may eventually be tried for the other killings that took place in different jurisdictions, this proceeding focused on only the murder of Dean Meyers, 53, at a

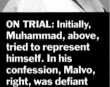

ON TRIAL: Initially, Muhammad, above, tried to represent himself. In his confession, Malvo, right, was defiant

gas station near Manassas, Va. Six days after the trial began, Muhammad unexpectedly dismissed his lawyers and took over his defense. Two days later, he changed his mind and reinstated his lawyers. The prosecution called 138 witnesses over several weeks; Malvo's team mounted a three-hour defense. On Nov. 17, the jury found Muhammad guilty on all charges. Two days later, jurors recommended that he receive the death penalty, but the judge will have the final say on the sentence. The first trial for Muhammad's alleged accomplice, John Lee Malvo, 18, is for the murder of Linda Franklin, 47, in Falls Church, Va. It began on Nov. 10.

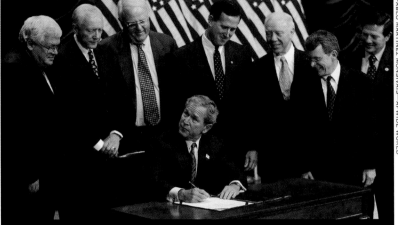

MAN'S WORLD: The President signs a bill outlawing some abortion procedures

The Year in Congress

The photograph above captures a moment of triumph for the White House—as well as a rare instance when the Administration's finely tuned imagemaking machinery went off-kilter. On Nov. 5, President Bush signed into law a bill, long sought by pro-life adherents, that criminalizes the procedure they term partial-birth abortion. But critics howled as they pointed out that the President's picture posse on this occasion included not a single woman—only seven white men. The bill passed both the House and Senate with solid majorities. In other legislative news:

Medicare On Nov. 25, the Senate passed a controversial bill that calls for the largest overhaul of the federal health program in its history. The bill includes a prescription drug benefit for seniors that will begin in 2006. But opponents argued it was a first step toward privatizing the federal program.

Energy A last-minute push to pass a comprehensive energy bill failed just before Thanksgiving. Critics claimed the bill was laden with pork to buy off legislators seeking projects for their districts.

Federal judges After a bitterly partisan debate in November, G.O.P. Senators were unable to override a Democratic threat to

filibuster, and the confirmation of four judges appointed to the federal bench by the President was blocked. Republicans cried foul, but Democrats pointed out that the G.O.P. had dished out the same treatment to a number of appointments made during Bill Clinton's presidency.

LOSING FACE: The Man, then and now

Farewell to the "Old Man"

The stern granite profile New Hampshire residents call "The Old Man of the Mountain" has long been the state's most recognized landmark. Carved naturally by a glacier some 30,000 years ago, the 40-ft. visage in Franconia Notch State Park has appeared on license plates, postage stamps and the state quarter. Alas! Early in May the Old Man crumbled, defying decades of efforts to preserve it.

A Dual Death in California

On Christmas Eve, 2002, Laci Peterson, 27, a mother-to-be with

Images

Nightclub Inferno

An estimated 350 fans of the '80s rock group Great White were packed into the Station, a cramped nightclub in West Warwick, R.I., on Feb. 20. As the band began its first song, "gerbs," sparking pyrotechnic fountains, shot up from the stage. Flames quickly crawled up a foam-covered wall and spread to the 9-ft.-high ceiling. The grim tally: 100 dead, more than 200 injured. A video camera caught the scene, at left.

admitted to having had an extramarital affair with Amber Frey, a masseuse. His trial was tentatively set to begin in late January.

SUSPICION: Scott Peterson, top right, was accused of the murder of wife Laci, center. Frey is at left

an infectious smile, disappeared from her home in Modesto, Calif. In April, police announced that the decomposed bodies of a small woman and full-term male fetus had washed up on a shoreline some 90 miles northwest of Modesto. Five days later, officials identified the victims as Laci and her child and arrested her husband Scott Peterson for their murder. He pleaded innocent, but later

Legislators on the Lam!

Politics doubles as entertainment in Texas: on May 11, in order to stymie a vote on redistricting that would send more Republicans to Congress, 51 out of 62 Democrats in the Texas legislature hightailed it out of Austin and holed up in Oklahoma. Not to be outdone, Democratic senators decided to visit enchanting New Mexico in June. It was all for naught: the Republicans pushed through their redistricting plan, in a major victory for Tom Delay, the powerful U.S.

AWOL: Yikes! Democrats at large

House leader from Texas whose office managed the effort.

Tragedy on the Ferry

Since 1884 the Staten Island Ferry has been carrying people across New York Harbor, offering a 25-min. trip that's gloriously picturesque (it passes the Statue of Liberty). And it's cheap: since 1977, the ride has been free. On Oct. 15, 10 people were killed and dozens injured when a ferry outbound from Manhattan plowed at high speed into a dock on Staten Island. The assistant captain fled the scene and attempted suicide. An inquiry is ongoing.

AFTERMATH: The shattered ferry is towed away

PORTFOLIO: **WAR IN IRAQ**

Pentagon officials were strongly criticized for keeping reporters and photographers far from the front during the first Gulf War in 1991. This time around, the military took a different tack, "embedding" journalists within its units and allowing them unprecedented access to the troops. As seen on the following pages, photojournalists responded with brilliant and moving images of two very different cultures at war

Best Face Forward

Carbine? Check. Combat boots? Check.
Q-tips? Check. Two weeks before the first
U.S. troops would invade Iraq, a soldier from
the 1st Marine Division starts the day with
a shave at a camp in northern Kuwait,
15 miles from the Iraqi border

Photograph for TIME by Robert Nickelsberg—Getty Images

On the Attack

On March 21, the first day of the ground war, a British Royal Marine from the 42 Commando group fires a wire-guided missile at an Iraqi position on the Faw peninsula. 11,000 British troops joined some 140,000 American ground forces in the "coalition of the willing" assembled by the U.S. to topple Saddam Hussein

Photograph by Jon Mills— Pool—Reuters—Landov

Hunkered Down

In the early days of the invasion, the spearhead of U.S. and British forces moving in from Kuwait encountered tougher-than-expected opposition in several key cities in southern Iraq, including Nasiriyah and Basra. Saddam's forces were aided by the weather, as a crippling sandstorm limited visibility and mobility. Soldiers slept and snacked on Skittles, waiting for the storm to lift

Photograph by James Hill—Getty Images

Orphan of the Storm

As the sandstorm raged, this Iraqi boy was stopped, along with two adult companions, by members of the U.S. Army's 3rd Infantry Division. Under attack by combatants dressed in civilian garb, American troops were stopping and frisking most Iraqis they encountered. The boy and his companions were released

Photograph for TIME by Christopher Morris—VII

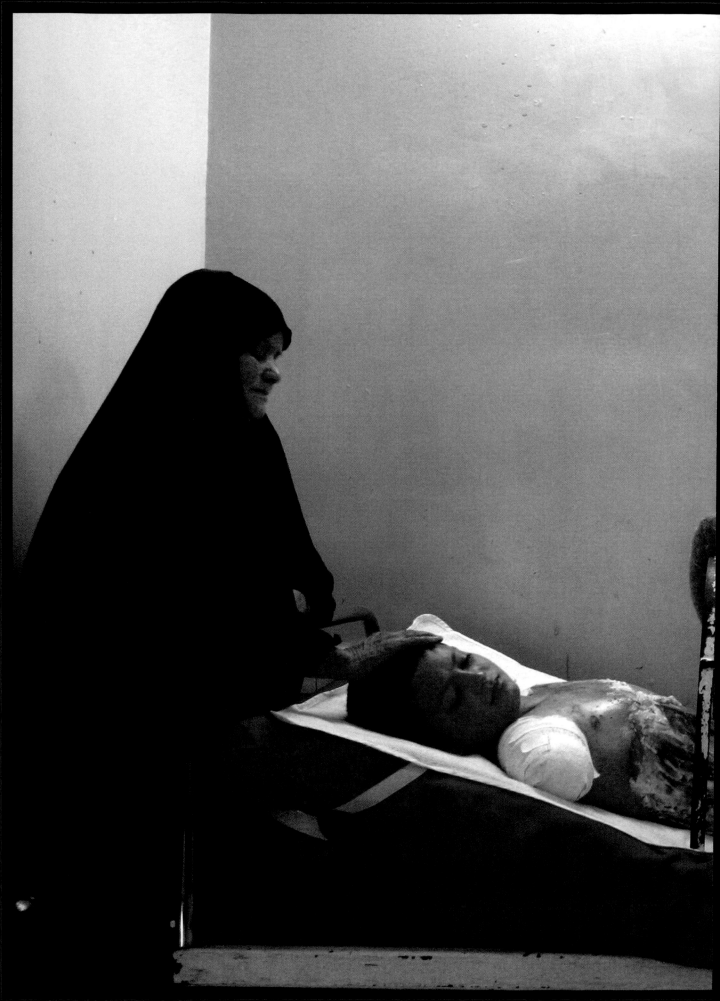

Collateral Damage

Ali Islamil Abbas, 12, lost both his arms and was severely burned after a missile hit his home south of Baghdad. At the time this picture was taken, he had not been told that his pregnant mother, stepfather, brother and six sisters had been killed in the attack. The woman comforting him is a distant aunt. The boy, who developed septicemia as a result of his burns, was later moved to another hospital, out of harm's way

Photograph for TIME by Yuri Kozyrev

Two snipers from the 101st Airborne Division comb through an abandoned Iraqi military building on the outskirts of Najaf, a major city southwest of Baghdad. After showing unexpectedly strong resistance to U.S. and British troops in the first days of the invasion, the Iraqi army collapsed quickly in the third week of the war

Photograph for TIME by Benjamin Lowy—Corbis

Baghdad Barbie? An Iraqi boy ponders an American icon painted on a wardrobe drawer, which was taken by his father from the villa of one of Saddam's relatives in the capital city. Looting was widespread in the lawless days following the collapse of Saddam's regime

Photograph for TIME by Yuri Kozyrev

With Saddam out of power, Iraq's Shi'ite Muslims were free for the first time in 35 years to make a pilgrimage to the holy city of Karbala, 35 miles southeast of Baghdad. Here they performed a ritual of self-mutilation that commemorates the 7th century slaying of Hussein, grandson of the Prophet Muhammad. A youngster joins in the frenzy as men slash their heads with daggers. Shi'ites, who make up some 60% of Iraq's population, were oppressed under Saddam's Sunni-led regime

Photograph for TIME by James Nachtwey—VII

Medic!

A U.S. Marine carries a wounded comrade while calling for aid
through his headset microphone during an Iraqi artillery attack
11 miles southeast of Baghdad. At least two Marines were killed in
this engagement during the last days of the ground war

Joyride

A U.S. Marine celebrates the collapse of Saddam's regime
by sliding down a marble banister in one of the Iraqi leader's
former palaces in Tikrit, his hometown. The soldier's glee was
premature; Tikrit, Mosul and other towns of the nation's
Sunni Triangle, north of Baghdad, continued to harbor resistance
fighters loyal to Saddam. U.S. troops trying to secure the
region took casualties for as long as six months after the major
combat phase of the war was declared over on May 1

Slaughter at a Shrine

A man screams for help after a bomb exploded outside the shrine
of Imam Ali in Najaf, 120 miles south of Baghdad, on Aug. 29. Among the
more than 80 people who died was Ayatullah Mohammed Bakir al-Hakim,
64, one of the nation's most senior Shi'ite clerics and a longtime foe of
Saddam Hussein. The cleric had returned to Iraq following Saddam's fall
after two decades in exile. The explosion in one of Iraq's holiest sites, and
the murder of a leading moderate religious leader, dealt a major blow
to the stability of the occupied nation, which is deeply divided
along political, ethnic and religious lines

A U.S. soldier rests in the wrecked lobby of the United Nations offices in Baghdad, destroyed by a suicide bomber on Aug. 19. Twenty-two people, including Sergio Vieira de Mello, the Brazilian head of the U.N.'s mission in Iraq, were killed in the blast; scores more were wounded. The successful attack, coming five months after the fall of Saddam's government, underscored the fragility of the U.S. occupation of Iraq

Photograph for TIME by Stephanie Sinclair—Corbis

BOMBS ALONG

FOR THE SECOND TIME IN 12 YEARS, AN ALLIED COALITION UNDER U.S. CONTROL UNLEASHE

FOR A MOMENT, THE ENTIRE WORLD SEEMED TO HOLD its breath. After months of tough talk and diplomatic feints, U.S. President George W. Bush issued an ultimatum on Monday, March 17: strongman Saddam Hussein and his two ruthless sons, Qusay and Uday, had 48 hours to leave Iraq, or the U.S. and its allies would wage a war to make them leave. But as the hours ticked by, the trio stayed put—while some 250,000 allied troops in the region rechecked their gear and the Pentagon put a final polish on its plans to bring "regime change" to Iraq's long-suffering people.

But then, hours before Bush's deadline was to expire (on Wednesday evening in Washington, early Thursday morning in Baghdad), U.S intelligence agencies came upon what promised to be one of those last-minute intelligence bonanzas that can change history. Saddam, his sons and many of Iraq's senior leaders, the spies told the President, were huddled together in three underground Baghdad bunkers. Almost instantly, the plan for the war's launch was switched from a spectacular "shock and awe" campaign—a massive air assault coupled with a rapid thrust of ground troops—to a surgically precise "decapitation strike" that promised to sweep Saddam and his henchmen from the stage with a single knockout punch.

Just before the sun rose over Baghdad on Thursday, Bush gave the go-ahead: three dozen Tomahawk missiles bearing 1,000-lb. warheads were fired from six warships in the Persian Gulf and Red Sea and slammed into the grounds of a private residence in Baghdad. Shortly after the missiles found their mark, clearing a path deep into the ground, a pair of U.S. F-117 fighters dropped four 2,000-lb. bunker-busting bombs on an underground facility believed to be sheltering Saddam and at least one of his sons.

Closely following this strike, the massive air-and-ground attack was launched. Before the sun rose, the skies over Baghdad were punctured with fire and thunder as

BAGHDAD On March 21, U.S. air strikes devastated hundreds of carefully selected military and government targets in the Iraqi capital. The "shock and awe" strike was the second salvo in the war to topple Saddam

THE TIGRIS

A WAR ON IRAQ. THE TARGET: DICTATOR SADDAM HUSSEIN'S REGIME

thousands of Tomahawk missiles and smart bombs crashed into their targets, sending balloons of searing orange flame aloft into the darkness. At the same time, U.S. troops crossed the border from Kuwait, piercing more than one-third of the way to Iraq's capital within 24 hours.

By morning, the smoke rose above Baghdad in plumes of thick, black soot, seeming to carry with it the ashes of a dying regime. But even days after the attempted decapitation strike, intelligence agencies remained unable to confirm that either Saddam or his sons had been killed. Then credible reports began to surface that all three were alive and in hiding. By Saturday, the mood at the White House and inside the war rooms of the allied coaltion had swung from hopeful expectation to stern sobriety as U.S. soldiers

began to encounter significant enemy fire outside southern Iraqi cities and on the road to Baghdad. "There's no cheering or high-fiving whatsoever," said a senior White House aide. "This is not a cakewalk."

For the second time in 12 years, American troops were fighting in Iraq. But if the 1991 Gulf War was characterized by a clearly explained and almost universally agreed-upon rationale and a set of specific, limited objectives that were quickly and neatly achieved, the sequel was distinguished by a questionable rationale, a definition of success that proved both changeable and elusive and a nonexistent exit strategy. The first Gulf War, waged by George W. Bush's father, had united both the American people and a surprisingly broad coalition of allies; the second war deeply divided

PABLO MARTINEZ MONSIVAIS—AP/WIDE WORLD

ON THE RECORD In his 2003 State of the Union address, Bush cited documents on Iraq's nuclear aims that proved false

had demonstrated its willingness to use such weapons against its own people (most notoriously in the aftermath of the 1991 war, while suppressing a Kurdish rebellion) and other nations (as it did against Iran during the 1980s).

But actual evidence that Saddam was still acting on this desire, more than a decade later, was hard to come by. In January 2003, U.N. inspectors reported, in essence, that while they couldn't find any proof that Iraq was still building weapons of mass destruction, neither could they find any proof that it wasn't. Yet in his 2003 State of the Union address that month, the President cited reports that Iraq had tried to buy weapons-grade uranium from Niger. These reports turned out to be unfounded, and critics later charged that U.S. intelligence agencies had known they were false even as the President used them as a justification for the war.

In making its case for war, the Bush Administration also pointed to Saddam's alleged links to the al-Qaeda terrorist network. But the White House's view on this point seemed somewhat fluid. It had denied that such links existed in the days after 9/11; then through most of 2002 it had allowed that some connection between Iraq and al-Qaeda might exist. By 2003, the suspicion had hardened into a conviction that Iraq had, as Bush said in his March 17 ultimatum to Saddam, "aided, trained and harbored terrorists, including operatives of al-Qaeda."

Bush also cited the promise of bringing democracy to one of the world's most brutal police states as a goal of the war, dismissing doubts, raised by political experts and historians, about whether a country that had never known democracy, in a region of the world with no democratic tradition, was fertile ground for government by the people. The nation's deep ethnic and religious divisions were often compared with those that turned once united Yugoslavia into a fragmented, factious group of warring states in the 1990s.

Behind every stated rationale for toppling Saddam, critics saw an unstated agenda—or smelled an oil well. Hawks like Deputy Defense Secretary Paul Wolfowitz and Penta-

Americans and split the U.S. from several major allies and from the United Nations, which refused to sanction it.

For the President and for the nation he led, the war represented a major gamble: it was based on a new strategy for the use of U.S. power, and it committed America to a deep, potentially lengthy involvement in the future of Iraq—the sort of "nation building" that George W. Bush had publicly scorned as a candidate for the presidency.

The campaign to topple Saddam reflected the shattering impact of the 9/11 attacks on America, for the President described it as an essential operation in the ongoing war on terrorism. Iraq was the first test case of a new, post-9/11 doctrine that called for pre-emptive strikes against foreign nations deemed to be a threat to U.S. security—an enormous shift in strategic direction for the world's only superpower. Bush's war against Saddam was a bold strategic initiative that could pay off with a new geopolitical order in the Middle East. But the downside was equally great: even if the military outcome of the war was little doubted, the price in division—both at home and around the world—could be lasting, and the length, cost and outcome of a U.S.-led occupation of Iraq were nagging questions.

Bush's reasons for demanding that Saddam be removed were compelling on their face but, said critics, short on specific, verifiable detail. The most important (and oft repeated) of these was the allegation that Iraq was building weapons of mass destruction. Indeed, Saddam's government had a long, well-documented history of trying to acquire or create both nuclear and biological munitions and

DIVIDED WE STAND

MARIO TAMA—GETTY IMAGES

UNITED STATES

GO IN! Powell lays out the rationale for the war at the U.N.

ON THE MARCH While residents smile from a doorway, U.S. soldiers from the 1st Marine Division enter Tharir on March 30

gon adviser Richard Perle had been advocating a new campaign in Iraq since shortly after the 1991 war ended, long before they came to power in a new Bush Administration. In the days and months following the 9/11 attacks, their views prevailed among some of the President's most influential advisers—including Vice President Dick Cheney and Secretary of Defense Donald Rumsfeld—and, finally, Bush himself.

A drumroll of events signaled the new policy. In Bush's 2002 State of the Union address, Iraq was named part of the "axis of evil." That June, in a major speech at the U.S. Military Academy at West Point, the President announced his new policy of pre-emptive engagement. Four months later, a Congressional resolution authorizing the use of force to remove Saddam drew strong bipartisan support. In January 2003, Bush ordered the military to prepare for war.

To this martial cadence, U.S. Secretary of State Colin Powell sought to build support for regime change in Iraq, making two major presentations to the U.N. in which he laid out the charges against Saddam. Britain, under Prime Minister Tony Blair, came onboard early. But longtime U.S. allies France and Germany found the arguments unpersuasive, as did U.N. heavyweights Russia and China. In January, France and Germany worked together to block a

In contrast to the first Gulf War in 1991, which was supported by the vast majority of Americans and attracted a broad coalition of allies, the 2003 war to bring regime change to Iraq split American opinion right down the middle and drove deep divisions between the U.S. and such major allies as Germany, France, Russia and China. Secretary of State Colin Powell's presentations on Iraq's weapons of mass destruction failed to persuade these nations and the United Nations Security Council to support the war. Meanwhile, America's streets filled with the largest protests in decades, and on Feb. 22 massive antiwar rallies were held around the globe. An unfazed George W. Bush said he would pay no attention to the protests, comparing them to advertising focus groups.

KEEP OUT! Protesters march in San Francisco in April, weeks after the war began

SEMPER FI On March 23, U.S. Marines in southern Iraq carry a wounded comrade, one of several injured when an Iraqi rocket-propelled grenade hit their vehicles outside Nasiriyah

"You've liberated a people ... you've deposed a cruel dictator." —DONALD RUMSFELD

U.S. plan under which NATO would assist Turkey in working with coalition troops against Iraq. At the same time, France called for a new round of tougher inspections that would have delayed the start of the war indefinitely.

In February, the U.S., joined by Britain and Spain, pressed for a Security Council resolution that would authorize the use of force against Iraq. Under threats of a veto by France, Germany, Russia and China, the resolution was withdrawn. Finally, on March 5, Powell said the U.S. would instead lead "a coalition of willing nations" to disarm Iraq with or without U.N. approval. The following day, Bush declared at a news conference that U.N. authorization was unnecessary, saying that "we really don't need anybody's permission" to defend U.S. interests. His ultimatum to Saddam followed quickly, and the clock counting down to the beginning of the war began ticking in Washington—and in Baghdad.

When Saddam didn't move, coalition forces did. The unsuccessful decapitation strike was followed by the "shock and awe" aerial and ground campaign, and troops barreled into Iraq. Within 24 hours, U.S. forces had captured the major oil fields in southern Iraq and had begun advancing on Baghdad. In the first week of the campaign, some of the fiercest resistance came not from Iraqi troops but from a desert sandstorm that grounded aircraft, blinded troops in the field and played havoc with the sensitive electronic gear that gives U.S. troops an edge over more crudely equipped combatants.

When the storm lifted, U.S. and British units that had advanced as far as the outskirts of Basra, Iraq's second largest city, faced resistance nearly as troublesome from units of the ambush-happy Fedayeen Saddam, a paramilitary force fanatically loyal to Saddam and his sons. This prompted a change in tactics for allied ground forces, which had been racing headlong toward Baghdad. Henceforth, forward units would advance more slowly, taking extra time to clear out concealed snipers and mortar positions.

On March 27, more than 1,000 U.S. airborne troops opened a second front by parachuting into the northern town of Harir, where they captured an air field. The days that followed saw the first major ground combat of the war as U.S.-led troops engaged in a series of pitched battles with Republican Guard forces in Hindiyah and Karbala, south of the capital. When these battles were over, the

Medina and Baghdad divisions of the Republican Guard had been destroyed, and U.S. forces were 25 miles from Baghdad. Organized resistance had now vanished; so had Saddam.

By April 4, American troops had captured Saddam International Airport, 10 miles from Baghdad. (It was soon renamed Baghdad International Airport.) Three days later, U.S. tanks were roaming at will through Baghdad, and British troops finally took the city of Basra. On April 9, ecstatic crowds in downtown Baghdad toppled a 40-ft.-tall statue of Saddam Hussein—with an assist from U.S. soldiers—and two days later, U.S. commanding general Tommy Franks declared that "the Saddam regime has ended."

What would come next and what the missing Saddam and his cohorts were up to were questions that, for the moment, were drowned out by the exuberant din of victory. Widespread looting and violent confrontations between angry Iraqi crowds and U.S. troops seemed to detract little from a conquest that had come more quickly and more cheaply than most had thought possible: the number of coalition dead was 169; the number of Iraqi dead was estimated at 3,000. As Rumsfeld told U.S. troops during an April 29 visit to Baghdad, "You've liberated a people, you've deposed a cruel dictator, and you have ended his threat to free nations."

But what was meant to be the last word on the war was uttered by Rumsfeld's superior, George W. Bush, who

SPOILS In the aftermath of the regime's fall, allied troops did little to stop a rampage of looting. Above, a Baghdad man bears Saddam's head in a barrow—a mini-decapitation strike

landed aboard the aircraft carrier U.S.S. *Abraham Lincoln* on May 1 and declared in a nationally televised speech—under a banner reading MISSION ACCOMPLISHED—that "major combat operations in Iraq have ended." The President went on to say, "In the battle of Iraq, the United States and our allies have prevailed. And now our coalition is engaged in securing and reconstructing that country." What it would take to accomplish this goal, how long the mission would last and whether it was even possible were questions that didn't seem pressing at that euphoric moment. Before long, they would be impossible to ignore. ■

WARRIOR Secretary of Defense Rumsfeld took a victory lap through Baghdad on April 30, where he was hailed by soldiers

AFTERMATH The day after the U.N. headquarters in Baghdad's Canal Hotel was bombed, killing 23, a team of U.S. Army Engineers reviews the damage

PEACE IS HELL

From the ashes of Saddam Hussein's dying regime a deadly campaign of insurgency is born. But the dictator's capture in December raises hopes for an end to the strife

ONE WEEK AFTER GEORGE W. BUSH DECLARED AN END to major combat operations in Iraq, Private First Class Marlin Rockhold, of Hamilton, Ohio, was directing traffic on a Baghdad bridge when he was shot and killed by a sniper. The same day, an Iraqi calmly walked up to another U.S. soldier on a second Baghdad bridge and shot him dead. Five days later, Air Force Sergeant Patrick Lee Griffin was killed when the convoy he was traveling in was ambushed by Iraqi insurgents. In the heady days after the U.S. declaration of victory, it was easy to dismiss these incidents and others like them as the inevitable winding down of a bloody conflict. But within weeks, a pattern of suicide bombings, sniper attacks and roadside ambushes began to emerge. The war may have been won, but someone forgot to inform the enemy.

Indeed, rather than trailing off, the attacks grew in frequency and ferocity in late May and early June, when 12 U.S. soldiers were slain over a three-week period. Perhaps more disturbing to military commanders, the attacks also grew in sophistication. What had begun as a series of random, sporadic actions increasingly resembled coordinated and carefully planned raids. By late June, Deputy Defense

Secretary Paul Wolfowitz was describing the ongoing conflict as a "guerrilla war." As if to prove him right, separate bands of Iraqi gunmen simultaneously attacked two allied troop detachments in the town of Majar al Kabir on June 24, killing six British soldiers.

The problems dashed the great expectations of U.S. planners and many Iraqi citizens: both groups seem to have imagined that once the war had been won, the country would recover from the devastation of battle in a matter of weeks, then quickly blossom into a free-market democracy. In reality, U.S. occupation authorities found it a struggle to police Iraq's streets, restore water and electricity, shore up the economy, rebuild schools, monitor local elections and nudge the country toward democracy—all while battling an increasingly brazen assortment of militants. Among the Iraqis, initial support for the occupiers began to give way to a growing sense that life had been better under the old regime. "At least we had power and security," said a Baghdad merchant. "Democracy is not feeding us."

By mid-July, the U.S. military estimated that American personnel in Iraq were coming under hostile fire an average of 12 times each day. Nor were occupying troops the only victims. Iraqis known to be cooperating with coalition forces were targeted for assassination: the U.S.-appointed mayor of Hadithah on July 17, the police chief of Khaldiya on Sept. 15 and the deputy mayor of Baghdad, along with a member of the U.S.-appointed Governing Council, in October. The pattern was clear.

Who was behind the attacks? Allied commanders ordered the Iraqi army to disband shortly after Baghdad fell. Yet declaring that an army no longer exists isn't the same thing as disarming it. Half a million unemployed soldiers walked Iraq's streets, many of them expected to care for extended families—after having received no pay for months—and many of them bearing weapons. Add to these disaffected citizens the extremists still loyal to the old regime, the Islamic fundamentalists who were oppressed by it and the "foreign fighters" reported to be sneaking into Iraq from around the Arab world, and the result was a highly combustible mix.

Army General John Abizaid (who took over the U.S. Central Command from Tommy Franks in July) declared in August, "It [the resistance] is getting more organized, and it is learning." The most dangerous area: the so-called Sunni triangle, north and west of Baghdad, heavily populated by Sunni Muslims like Saddam. The region included his hometown of Tikrit, where support for the deposed dictator ran deepest.

The attacks kept ratcheting up, both in scale and in the selection of strategic targets: now international organizations and the few U.S. allies in the coalition began to come under fire. On Aug. 7, a car bomb exploded outside the Jordanian embassy in Baghdad, killing 19 people. Twelve days later, a suicide bomber drove a truck loaded with explosives into the United Nations headquarters in Baghdad, killing 23 people, including the U.N.'s senior representative in Iraq, Sergio Vieira de Mello. On Aug. 29, another car bomb killed more than 80 people in Najaf, including the Ayatullah Mohammed Bakir al-Hakim, a moderate cleric who supported the occupation. On Oct. 27 (the first day in the Muslim holy month of Ramadan), five simultaneous suicide bombings in Baghdad targeted the headquarters of the Red Cross and four police stations, killing 35.

The next day marked a somber milestone: two U.S. soldiers died when their tank struck a bomb in Baqubah, 40 miles north of Baghdad. The number of U.S. losses to enemy action since the end of major combat operations now surpassed the total killed during the main conflict.

By the fall, criticism of President Bush and his strategy was growing. The failure of allied inspectors to find weapons of mass destruction—whose alleged presence had been one of the main arguments for the invasion—sapped public confidence. Polls showed steady erosion in Americans' support for the mission; Bush's approval ratings also softened. The heat on the President was turned up when he requested an $87 billion spending package for the occupation and reconstruction effort, in addition to the $62 billion allocated only six months before.

JESSICA LYNCH, SOLDIER

When U.S. Army Private First Class Jessica Lynch, recuperating in a military hospital in Germany, was well enough to speak, she had one question for her doctors: Had her story made the newspaper in Palestine, W.Va., the one-store hamlet in the Appalachian foothills where Lynch had spent nearly all her 19 years?

In a word: yes. After Army Rangers and Navy SEALs snatched her from an Iraqi hospital miles behind enemy lines, Lynch's story captivated the world. She was the subject of countless newspaper stories, a high-profile book and a TV movie that conveniently filled in factual blanks with heroism and flag waving. Lynch was an easy, remarkably apt symbol for ... well, for all the things that demand symbolizing in wartime.

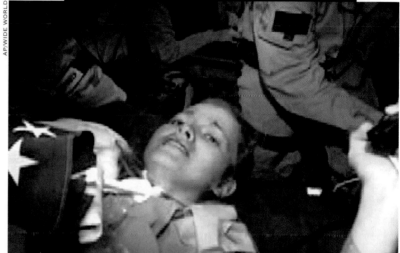

But the facts in her story proved hazy. Initial reports that Lynch had bravely fought off Iraqis until she ran out of ammo gave way to her own admission that her weapon was jammed with sand. Early versions of the tale that had rescuers bravely fighting through Iraqi Republican Guards to snatch her were revised to say the hospital was unguarded, nearly empty. What is indisputable is the trauma Lynch endured: two broken legs, a broken arm and massive back injuries. She appears to have been raped while she was a prisoner.

Captured, injured and rescued, Lynch was a hero when the Pentagon needed good news about a hard war. And she was "good copy" when media outlets needed to put a face on that war. But mostly she was Jessica Lynch, a teenage girl who was voted Miss Congeniality in the beauty pageant at her county fair and joined the Army to earn college tuition so she could teach kindergarten. To her credit, Lynch never lied about her experiences and politely recused herself from the Pentagon's starmaking machinery. To its credit, the Army owned up to the factual errors in its early stories about her. Lynch is home again; her recuperation may take two years. "God saved me," she says. "I feel lucky that I am here." Amen.

BLACKHAWK DOWN On Oct. 25, one U.S. helicopter is crippled and another is airborne, carrying survivors, outside U.S.-occupied Tikrit in the Sunni triangle

"[The resistance] is getting more organized, and it is learning." —U.S. GENERAL JOHN ABIZAID

Critics compared the situation with the Vietnam War, called the occupation a quagmire in the making and blasted Bush and his advisers for their rosy predictions that Iraqis would welcome allied troops as liberators. Bush's supporters responded by chiding the media for focusing only on negative reports from Iraq, citing thousands of everyday success stories they said would add up to victory in the battle to win the hearts and minds of Iraqis.

But on the ground the situation was still deadly. On Nov. 2, a missile attack near Fallujah brought down an Army CH-47 Chinook transport helicopter, killing 16 U.S. soldiers. Twelve days later, a rocket-propelled grenade hit a Black Hawk helicopter, which collided in mid-air with a second Black Hawk, killing 17 U.S. soldiers.

There were political missteps as well. Postwar planning was put under the control of the Pentagon, which named retired General Jay Garner (administrator of the "safe haven" area of northern Iraq after the 1991 Gulf War) to manage reconstruction. He floundered and was replaced by veteran diplomat Paul Bremer at the end of May. Bremer focused on basics (like turning the lights back on and reducing lines at the gas pump), while also trying to forge Iraq's squabbling leaders into something like a government. Said a British government official of the U.S. occupation: "It appears that there was no planning whatsoever."

By mid-November, however, the Bush Administration had a plan. On Nov. 15, Bremer presented the 25 members of the coalition-appointed Governing Council with a new timetable that called for local town meetings to select members of a transitional assembly, which would then elect a new provisional government. A general election would be scheduled for late 2005. Washington liked the plan, in part because it would technically end the role of U.S. occupation troops in time for the 2004 U.S. presidential elections. But while the formal transfer of power to

Iraqis would change the status of foreign troops from occupiers to allies, it wouldn't translate into an early exit for coalition forces; they seemed to be in for a long haul.

On the political front, the Bush Administration racked up a hat trick during eight days in October: on the 16th, the U.N. Security Council unanimously passed a resolution that legitimized the U.S. occupation —for now; on the 17th, Congress enacted the controversial $87 billion funding measure to cover occupation expenses; on the 24th, an international donor conference pledged $33 billion from more than 15 nations toward the cost of reconstruction.

Yet such victories paled next to the growing body count. With Americans more and more skeptical over the course of events, the White House needed to change the message, and it did so with a dramatic clandestine mission. On Nov. 27 the President surprised U.S. soldiers by flying secretly into Baghdad aboard a darkened Air Force One, landing in time to serve Thanksgiving dinner to 600 G.I.s. "I was just looking for a warm meal somewhere," he joked to stunned troops. The daring gesture provided a badly needed boost to G.I. morale: November had been the deadliest single month for coalition forces since the war began.

But for both Iraqis and Americans, the real occasion for giving thanks came unexpectedly, in mid-December, when U.S. forces captured Saddam Hussein. The arrest was good news for most Iraqis, putting an end to any chance they would ever again live under his rule. It raised a host of questions as well. Who would try the despot—and where? Would his arrest quell the insurgency or fuel it? Would Bush again reach out to major European allies to help reconstruct Iraq—and how would they respond? In Winston's Churchill's formulation, the capture of Saddam might be the end of the beginning of the U.S. adventure in Iraq—or it might be the beginning of the end. In the distinction between the two, many lives hung in the balance. ∎

THE FALL OF THE HOUSE OF SADDAM

A
♠

SADDAM HUSAYN AL-TIKRITI
President

ENDGAME Saddam was a bearded, defeated fugitive when captured in a small hole, ventilated by a fan, on a former aide's farm outside Tikrit

One of history's great tyrants, Saddam Hussein liked to portray himself as the heir to the legendary Saladin, the Arab leader who defeated the Crusaders. With the spoils of his rule, Saddam built more than 50 magnificent palaces around Iraq, and he dreamed that his sons Uday and Qusay would carry on his dynasty. But like so many megalomaniacs before him, Saddam saw his dreams turn to dust. When he was captured by U.S. troops on Dec. 13, he was a bearded, haggard fugitive—his chariot a taxicab, his palace an 8-ft.-deep spider hole. And his two sons had been dead for months, killed by coalition forces.

Soon after the fall of Baghdad, the U.S. Central Command in Iraq put the faces of the 55 most-wanted Iraqis from Saddam's regime on decks of playing cards and distributed them to occupying troops. The ace of spades was Saddam; the second and third cards in the deck were his two sons, whose reputation for torture, rape and thuggery stretched back to the 1980s. On July 22, acting on a tip, U.S. troops cornered Uday and Qusay at a private home in U.S.-occupied Mosul. When the troops asked to search the house, Uday and Qusay—along with a bodyguard and Qusay's 14-year-old son Mustafa—unleashed a withering barrage of gunfire. After a four-hour firefight, all four Iraqis were dead.

But where was Saddam? The man who had escaped decapitation strikes and rockets and satellites and bribes was nowhere to be found, even as the insurgency grew more deadly and more focused. As the months dragged on, U.S. forces centered the search on the region around Saddam's hometown of Tikrit, north of Baghdad, where loyalty among those who benefited most from his rule ran deep.

On Dec. 13, a team of 600 soldiers from the 4th Infantry Division and U.S. special forces acted on a tip that Saddam was hiding in a little town called Dawr, 15 miles from Tikrit. At 8:00 p.m. local time, they closed in on their prize, spreading out across two locations, labeled Wolverine One and Wolverine Two. The target: a farm owned by Qais al-Mameq, a former personal attendant of Saddam's. Initially, the search proved fruitless. But the troops kept at it, knowing Saddam's reputation for tunnels and safe rooms and secrets. On the premises there was a small, walled compound with a mud hut and a metal lean-to. There the U.S. troops found the entrance to a hole, camouflaged with dirt and bricks, covered with a Styrofoam lid. Inside, like a pharaoh in his tomb, was Saddam, surrounded with symbols of his lost power—two AK-47s, a pistol and $750,000 in U.S. $100 bills—the Butcher of Baghdad with pictures of Ben Franklin.

Saddam's captors scraped his throat, checked his teeth and took him to a secure location, where four members of Iraq's Governing Council identified him, and DNA tests were also performed. There was no doubt: as occupation chief Paul Bremer declared in kicking off a news conference hours later: "Ladies and gentlemen … We got him."

Saddam's capture set off celebratory gunfire in Baghdad and electrified Americans on a Sunday morning when most folks had little more than football games and holiday shopping on their agenda. A restrained George W. Bush addressed the nation at noon, reminding citizens of both Iraq and the U.S. that the capture of the dictator did not mean that the resistance to the U.S.-led occupation would end. Indeed, Saddam's condition when he was taken suggested that he had little direct control over the insurgents.

The capture silenced, if only for the moment, Bush's critics at home and abroad. And in putting to rest forever the possibility of Saddam's return to power, it might help stabilize Iraq—for you can't bring peace to a haunted house.

THUGS Uday, right, the older and more brutal of Saddam's sons, survived an assassination attempt in 1996. Qusay, the younger of the two, was being groomed to succeed Saddam

PERSON OF

THE
AMERICAN
SOLDIER

THE YEAR

BY NANCY GIBBS

MODERN HISTORY HAS A WAY OF being modest with its gifts and blunt with its reckonings. Good news comes like a breeze you feel but don't notice; the markets are up, the air is cleaner, we're beating heart disease. It is the bad news that comes with a blast or a crash, to stop us in midsentence to stare at the TV, and shudder.

NIGHT WATCH: Sergeant Marquette Whiteside of the Survey Platoon, Headquarters Battery, a.k.a. the Tomb Raiders, on patrol in Baghdad

Photographs for TIME by James Nachtwey—VII

SEEKING COVER After hearing fire, Sergeant Michael Hughson uses a vehicle as a shield in front of the Abu Hanifa mosque, the heart of Adhamiya district

Maybe that's why Americans were startled by gratitude when Saddam Hussein was captured on Dec. 13: pulling the fugitive from his hole in the ground suggested the possibility of pulling an entire country out of the dark. In an exhausting year when we witnessed battles well beyond the battlefields—in the streets, in our homes, with our allies—to share good news felt like breaking a long fast, all the better since it came by surprise. And who delivered this gift, against all odds and risks? The same citizens who shared the duty of living with, and dying for, a country's most fateful decisions. Scholars can debate whether the Bush Doctrine is the most muscular expression of national interest in a half-century; the generals may ponder whether warmaking or peacekeeping is the more fearsome assignment; civilians will remember a winter wrapped in yellow ribbons and duct tape. But in a year when it felt at times as if we had nothing in common anymore, we were united in this hope: that our men and women at arms might soon come safely home, their job done. They were the bright, sharp instrument of a blunt policy, and success or failure in a war unlike any in history ultimately rested with them.

For uncommon skills and service, for the choices each one of them has made and the ones still ahead, for the challenge of defending not only our freedoms but those barely stirring half a world away, the American soldier is TIME's Person of the Year 2003.

TIME followed a single platoon from the Army's 1st Armored Division, to watch its life on the line and glimpse what the world's largest army can do while the expectations for it are changing. There is no such thing as a typical platoon, but every one has stories to tell, about the costs of war and the price of peace and what you learn getting from one to the next. In the following pages, we tell four such stories.

It is worth remembering that our pilots and sailors and soldiers are, for starters, all volunteers, in contrast to most nations, which conscript those who serve in their armed forces. Ours are on duty in 146 countries, from Afghanistan to Zimbabwe. The 1.4 million men and women on active duty make up the most diverse military in our history, and yet it is not exactly a mirror of the country it defends. It is better educated than the general population and over-weighted with working-class kids and minorities. About 40% of the troops are Southern, 60% are white, 22% are black, and a disproportionate number come from empty states like Montana and Wyoming. When they arrive at the recruiter's door, Defense Secretary Donald Rumsfeld told TIME, "they have purple hair and an earring, and they've never walked with another person in step in their life. And suddenly they get this training, in a matter of weeks, and they become part of a unit, a team. They're all sizes and shapes, and they're different ages, and they're different races, and you cannot help when you work with them but come away feeling that that is really a special thing that this country has."

The unstated promise is that soldiers are sent to war only as a last resort, to defend their country from harm. But while the threat posed by Saddam was chief among the stated justifications, George W. Bush's war was always about more than the weapons that have yet to be found. The son of the President who had trouble with the Vision Thing offered a vision so broad it bent the horizon: this was nothing less than a "battle for the future of the Muslim world," an expression of American idealism in all its arrogant generosity. Once again, we thought we could liberate a country just by walking in the door. The President could move this immense fighting machine halfway around the world, and call old allies cowards who don't stand for anything, for leaving it to us to rescue a captive country.

If diplomacy normally involves the disguising of discord, Bush's policy meant inflaming it: NATO and the U.N. were divided; so was our own government, as State, the Pentagon and the CIA grappled in a three-way tug-of-war. One Marine, training in Kuwait's northern desert and waiting for war to begin, wondered whether protesters would spit on him when he came home. But for all the dissension, no one was blaming the soldiers: antiwar demonstrators argued they were fighting to defend our troops against an ill-conceived mission based on distorted intelligence. Even Howard Dean, whose antiwar campaign ambushed the Democratic Party, criticized Bush for asking too much of the nation's soldiers and reserves and diverting attention from more imminent threats.

It may be that idealism requires naiveté to survive, because no war ever goes as planned, and peace can be just

scan from head to toe before flashing the light onto his wristwatch and humming softly. The Iraqi, perhaps convinced that his thoughts and secrets had been electronically captured in a Casio, would often confess.

Of course, there are no magic bullets, and it isn't what the soldiers carry that determines whether they win the day; it's who they are and who they have become. The fight for peace demands different skills of the soldiers: not just courage but constancy; not just strength but subtlety. Liberty can't be fired like a bullet into the hard ground. It requires, among other things, time and trust, and a nation scarred by tyranny and divided by tribe and faith is not going to turn into Athens overnight. A force intensely trained for its mission finds itself improvising at every turn, required to exercise exquisite judgment in extreme circumstances: Do you shoot the 8-year-old when he picks up the grenade launcher? How do you win the hearts and minds of residents in a town you've had to wrap in barbed wire? How do you teach about freedom through the bars of a cage?

It is a fantastically romantic notion, that thousands of young men and women could descend on a broken place and make it better, not decades from now but right away, hook up the high school Internet lab, send the Army engineers to repair the soccer field, teach the town council about *Robert's Rules* and all the while watch your back. They debate how much to tell their loved ones back home, who listen to each news report of victories won and lives lost with the acute attention that dread demands. They complain less about the danger than the uncertainty: they are told they're going home in two weeks, and then two months later they have not moved.

THE FIGHT FOR PEACE DEMANDS DIFFERENT SKILLS
OF THE SOLDIERS: NOT JUST COURAGE BUT CONSTANCY;
NOT JUST STRENGTH BUT SUBTLETY

as confounding. The same soldiers who swept across 350 miles in 21 days, to be greeted by flowers and candy and cheers as the statues fell, soon found themselves being shot at by the people they had come to save. As it turned out, the Iraqi civil servants who were supposed to keep the lights on after Saddam was gone instead stayed home when there was no one to give them orders. The sudden collapse of the Iraqi army was such an indignity to the Iraqi people that in a way it made the Americans' job harder: You can rebuild a bridge, but how do you restore national pride at the same time, or impose order on a country that seems hard-wired to resist it?

The campaign of shock and awe was always aimed at mind and heart: many Iraqis viewed America as magically powerful, which raised their hopes and, in some cases, broke their will to resist. One U.S. soldier, when raiding a house in search of weapons, would aim his cheap key-ring flashlight at the scalp of a suspect, then

When the Pentagon announced that instead of six months abroad the troops would be spending a year, it began rotating them home for a two-week leave to rest and recharge. Some turned the offer down; they said it would be too hard to go back when the 14 days were up. Some went home to meet their babies for the first time. They flush the toilet over and over, just because they can, celebrate a year's worth of birthdays in 14 days, meet the new neighbors, savor rain. Troops come home to a Heroes' Parade: towns don't call it a Victory Parade, because they know it's not over yet.

It now falls to the Iraqis themselves to decide what they are willing and able to do with the chance they have been given, and the rest of the world to decide how to help. Freedom's consequences, intended and otherwise, will determine whether the world is safer for having been forcibly rearranged, and how long it will be before the soldiers can come marching home for good.   ■

DREAM, REALITY
Backed by beauties, Whiteside cleans his light machine gun

PORTRAITS FROM A PLATOON

OVERWORKED, UNDER FIRE, NERVOUS, PROUD, U.S. SOLDIERS FROM A FIELD ARTILLERY SURVEY PLATOON IN THE ARMY'S 1ST ARMORED DIVISION TRY TO STAY ALIVE IN A RUGGED BAGHDAD DISTRICT. HERE ARE FOUR TALES OF THEIR LIVES—AND OF THEIR FAMILIES BACK HOME

SGT. MARQUETTE WHITESIDE, 24

WAR AGES A ROGUISH SON

Catherine Whiteside is flipping through an old photo album, looking for a newspaper clipping of her eldest son, Marquette, winning a 4-H honor as a teenager. She stops to laugh at a picture of him in his "bushy" phase, when his hair was pretty much standing on end. Mother and son are close. People often think they're a couple because she looks so young at 42. "You know what he did while he was with the Army in Germany?" she asks mischievously. "He was dancing, stripping, under the name Scissor."

She dubbed him Sizzle instead, just to rib him, and the nickname stuck. That's how he signed his letters home from Baghdad. His early missives have the tone of a jokester writing to a friend, not to a worried mom back in Pine Bluff, Ark. They open with "Dear Chocolate"—his name for her—and include macho tales of his refusal to duck while under fire, followed by admonitions not to worry. He cracks jokes about how insurgents once lobbed rockets at his unit's base as the soldiers slept. "My son," says Catherine, "has a weird sense of humor."

▶ **HOME FRONT**
Whiteside's mother and daughter with a photo of dad Marquette

Marquette's correspondence took a more sober tone in November after a humvee in which he was riding was hit by a roadside bomb; his revered platoon leader lay mortally wounded in his arms. Now he e-mails home almost daily, often to confide about his nightmares. He keeps replaying the image of his dead lieutenant with a bloody gash where an eye should have been. Catherine knows about fear. She is a beat cop in a town of 55,000 where the crime rate is double the national average. "I know I could get shot at, but he's living it every day."

Marquette was due to come home in early 2004. But without telling his mother, he signed up for three more years in the Army. He has been promised a six-month break between tours of duty, but his mother is worried his luck will run out before he returns. After U.S. troops arrested Saddam Hussein on Dec. 13, a bullet narrowly missed Marquette's head while he was on patrol in Baghdad. "He says it's worse now," says Catherine.

Asked how she's holding up, Catherine picks up a prescription bottle of Zoloft from the coffee table and checks the date. September. That's when she found out that Marquette had re-upped and that the youngest of her three children, Shamario, 18, also a soldier, would be going to Iraq early in 2004. Then she saw a photo of Marquette in Baghdad that was posted on an online site for African Americans. The shot—of a thinner, older-looking Marquette—scared her. "I had to take a stress leave. He usually smiles all the time. He looked so sad." For two weeks she lay in bed, watching TV, fixated on the war.

She is angry now, angry that the war might claim two of her children. "Every time I see the President, I turn from him. There's nothing he can say unless he says he's bringing all the kids home."

On weekends Catherine takes care of Brashawn, Marquette's 6-year-old daughter by an ex-girlfriend. It's all very normal, says Catherine, except for the part where they e-mail Marquette to tell him to stay safe. There's an awkward silence, then she starts thumbing through the album again. She had looked forward to her son's coming home permanently, and now she will have two in harm's way. "I thought it was over." she says. "All over."

DOWNTIME: Grimes on her bunk. One plus to being female: her own room

SPC BILLIE GRIMES, 26

A ROLE MODEL FOR BABY BROTHER

Specialist Christopher Grimes, 25, has a favorite story about his big sister Billie, now a medic stationed in Iraq. For a time, when Christopher was in middle school in their hometown of Lebanon, Ind., an older boy would routinely walk up to him as he was finding a place to sit on the bus and shove him into a seat. Christopher never responded. But Billie, then a high school freshman who rode the same bus, couldn't take it. "Finally, she got tired of it, and she just stood up and clocked him," Christopher recalls. "That's the kind of person she is. When it comes to family, that's what comes first."

Their parents Bill and Wanda Grimes weren't thrilled when Billie's smack-the-knave impulses propelled her into the Army. She coped with their resistance to her ambition by simply not telling them when she joined the reserves in college. She liked it so much, she signed up for active duty after graduating. Christopher followed her lead, though their parents also opposed his enlistment. Now, with Billie in Baghdad, Wanda, 46, finds herself tensing up every morning at 6, the traditional time that families are notified of military casualties. She and her husband begin and end each day with a prayer that Billie will remain safe. "I can't go every day as the tough guy,"

A TIGHT DUO
Christopher and Billie before her deployment. He is heading to Iraq

says Bill, 46, a printer and former member of the Air Force security police. "We've tried to put it in God's hands."

Still, the Grimeses say they experience almost paralyzing fear every time a U.S. soldier dies in Iraq, then gut-wrenching guilt over their relief it wasn't Billie. They avoid the news whenever possible. Wanda's worst moment was seeing, on CNN, a still smoking armored ambulance that had been hit with a rocket-propelled grenade in Baghdad. The vehicle was just like the one Billie drives. "It was all I could do to hold it together and not become hysterical at work," says Wanda, a nurse.

Their worries will multiply when Christopher, an MP who served in Afghanistan for six months, ships out for Iraq in March. Billie has told Christopher, who is based at Fort Bragg in North Carolina and has a wife, Jacque, and a 15-month-old daughter, Stacia, that she would rather he not come to Iraq. Christopher has been well briefed on conditions there by his sister. A fan of fellow Indianan David Letterman, Billie sends home Top 10 lists like "Top 10 Reasons Prison Is Better Than Serving in Iraq." Among them: better gyms, showers, meals that don't contain chicken, and "not being shot at while you work."

Wanda and Bill at least have found a productive outlet for their anxieties: they helped organize a church group that sends letters and care packages to soldiers in Iraq. "It's helped us direct our energies," Bill says. "We're doing something instead of just sitting around feeling sorry for ourselves."

SECOND LIEUT. BEN COLGAN

A BIG EMPTY SPACE LEFT BEHIND

Jill Asay fell in love with Ben Colgan on their first date in New York City when, in a burst of exuberance, he suddenly started running down First Avenue, hurdling parking meters. Struck by the sight, other men on the street began imitating Ben. Though some were taller than his 5 ft. 7 in., none could clear the meters. "That was my moment," recalls Jill, 34. "Here's this guy: he's athletic, he's fun, but mostly he's a leader. He made other guys want to follow him."

Colgan's relatives also talk about his charisma. When he was a boy growing up in Kent, Wash., he was the Pied Piper, as his mother Pat calls him, to his friends and seven siblings.

There is the story of Ben's breaking his wrist on his first attempt to ride a bull and still persuading his younger brother to ride. And of his crashing a party at which friends predicted he would get roughed up and then calling from inside to report on the new pals he had made.

The Colgans are having to adjust now to the large empty space in their lives that Ben's death has created. On Nov. 2, the 30-year-old lieutenant died in Baghdad after his humvee was hit by a roadside bomb. Ben's parents are trying to come to grips with losing a son to a war they were against. Longtime peace activists, the couple marched against the idea of going to

war in Iraq. His father Joe says the family was always united in support of Ben, and once the war actually started the family stopped debating it. Joe adds that he has forgiven the person who took his son's life: "They are fighting for their country just like we are fighting for ours."

Ben's widow displays no anger over the loss of her husband. "Joining the military is voluntary," Jill says. "He felt lucky to be an American and wanted to be part of making a difference. He died doing what he wanted to be doing." Some days, she acknowledges, "I want to curl up and cry and be miserable." But

she adds, "I can't. They need me." *They* are the couple's three daughters: Grace, 2, Paige, 1, and baby Cooper, who arrived Dec. 19. Grace is old enough to know something is amiss. "She still asks about Ben all the time," says Jill, who tells the tiny blond her father is in heaven.

REMEMBERING Ben in Iraq in October, above. Below right, the Colgans' 2002 Christmas card. Below, a pregnant Jill with the girls after Ben's death

ESCAPE ARTIST
Beverly's wall served as canvas for a Spider-Man sketch

In the six months Ben was in Iraq, Jill compiled a trove of letters, e-mails, photos and audiocassettes from her husband, who taped himself reading stories and singing made-up songs for his daughters. "I'm grateful he died the way he did," says Jill of his tour of duty. "If it was a car wreck, we wouldn't have all these mementos. I've got all this to share with his girls."

On the day in May that Ben's unit deployed from its German base to Iraq, Jill left Germany too, moving

in with her father and step-mother in Aurora, Mo. She plans to remain there but will spend time also in Washington State with Ben's extended family, whom she's counting on "to help keep his memory alive for his children."When Ben was born in February 1973, his parents, following a family tradition, planted a tree, a lace-leaf maple, in their yard in Kent. A black ribbon now hangs on the tree's barren branches, next to the yellow one the Colgans had attached earlier in the hopes he would return safely from Iraq.

PFC JIM BEVERLY, 19

A PURPLE HEART AND A TICKET OUT

This is not what a mother wants to hear on the phone from her son serving in the Army in Iraq: "Well, I got my Purple Heart." Those words, delivered in a morphine slur, gave life to Jocelyn Perge's second worst nightmare about her son Jim Beverly. Perge's ex-husband Charles Beverly felt his stomach drop when he got the same call from Jim, who had suffered shrapnel wounds to his face, hand and knee in a Dec. 10 grenade attack on a humvee. Then, Charles recalls, he experienced a powerful sense of relief. "He was on the phone, talking to me," he says of his son. "He's alive."

Jocelyn, 47, a first-grade teacher in Akron, Ohio, had opposed Jim's enlistment. His entire senior year of high school, he had talked about following his father and grandfather into the service. But because he was only 17 when he graduated, Jim needed both parents' permission to sign up. Thinking her son was just going through a phase, Jocelyn refused. She still "was in denial," she says, when he joined the Army two days after turning 18. Nonetheless, she says, "I'm proud of him for doing what he believed in." Although Jocelyn opposes the war, she never leaves the house without her gold star, a pin distributed by a local bank in support of the troops. Jim's father, a Vietnam veteran, was always enthusiastic about his son's enlistment. "It's an

BOY SOLDIER
Beverly, who turned 19 in Iraq, posed for a portrait before his deployment

excellent idea for the education. You play the odds and figure they were in your favor," says Charles, 53, district manager for a photography company in Youngstown, Ohio.

Jocelyn confesses that once she was assured Jim's life was not in danger, she was worried the shrapnel had permanently disfigured her handsome son. "I know it's ridiculous," she says. "He's alive." Charles says he knows that Jim, who will spend Christmas 2003 recuperating in Akron, has the strength to prevail over this setback.

Both parents speak of Jim's sense of humor, and a creative bent that helps him escape. He likes to sketch characters from computer games and has a particular fondness for *Lara Croft, Tomb Raider*. His mother was surprised—and pleased—to learn his unit is called the Tomb Raiders. "That seems so appropriate for him," she says. Jim, who wants to become a journalist, has sketched characters and fantasy figures since childhood. He's good enough that his training unit at boot camp had him design a bulldog logo for their T shirts. Jocelyn knows he's running low on drawing supplies when she receives the rare letter home, asking for more colored pencils and notebooks. Jim also "draws a mean Sonic," another computer-game character that's a favorite of her first-graders. The kids know Jocelyn's son is in the war, and "they ask all the time if he's O.K.," she says. At Thanksgiving, the children brought her turkey drawings they had made for him. When she told them Jim had been hurt, they started making get-well cards. "I like being around them," she says. "It's comforting."

WHO THEY ARE

PERSONNEL

The **ARMY** is the largest of the armed forces. Its percentage of blacks is more than double that of the national population

RACE
White	58.4%
Black	26.3%
Hispanic	8.9%
Other	6.4%

SEX
Men	84.5%
Women	15.5%

RANK
Enlisted	84.1%
Officers	13.6%
Warrant officers	2.3%

AGE
0 10 20 30 40 5

17 to 19
20 to 24
25 to 29
30 to 34
35 to 39
40 to 44
45 to 49
50 and over

Enlisted
Office

The **NAVY** had the highest percentage of minority recruits last year, 43%. Overall, 37% of sailors are minorities

RACE
White	62.8%
Black	19.0%
Hispanic	9.7%
Other	8.5%

SEX
Men	85.9%
Women	14.1%

RANK
Enlisted	85.5%
Officers	14.0%
Warrant officers	0.5%

AGE
0 10 20 30 40 5

17 to 19
20 to 24
25 to 29
30 to 34
35 to 39
40 to 44
45 to 49
50 and over

Enlist
Offic

The **AIR FORCE** has the highest percentage of women in the military, and has the smallest percentage of minorities

RACE
White	75.5%
Black	16.2%
Hispanic	5.0%
Other	3.3%

SEX
Men	80.8%
Women	19.2%

RANK
Enlisted	80.6%
Officers	19.4%

AGE
0 10 20 30 40

17 to 19
20 to 24
25 to 29
30 to 34
35 to 39
40 to 44
45 to 49
50 and over

Enlis
Offic

The **MARINE CORPS** has the highest percentage of males in the services and the youngest average age

RACE
White	67.9%
Black	15.0%
Hispanic	13.1%
Other	4.0%

SEX
Men	93.9%
Women	6.1%

RANK
Enlisted	89.9%
Officers	9.0%
Warrant officers	1.1%

AGE
0 10 20 30 40

17 to 19
20 to 24
25 to 29
30 to 34
35 to 39
40 to 44
45 to 49
50 and over

Enlis
Offic

FAMILY

RESERVES

Slightly more than half of **ARMY** personnel are married, and just under half have children. On average, soldiers are just over 24 years old at the birth of their first child

MARITAL STATUS

Married 51.5%
Unmarried 48.5%

Percentage married to other service members: **11%**

Women married to other service members: **17.8%**

Men married to other service members: **3.2%**

CHILDREN

Have children 47.1%
Have no children 52.9%

Both parents in the military: **12,000**

Single parent: **36,000**

The Army Reserve has the highest percentage of minority officers, 25%

46% of Army Reserve and 52% of National Guard members are married. Very few reservists—1.6%—are married to another service member

30% of reservists have children. The average age at which reservists have their first child is relatively high: 27 in the Army National Guard and 35 in the Army Reserve

5.5% are single parents

The **NAVY** has the lowest percentage of members married to another person in the military as well as the highest percentage of single parents

■ **MARITAL STATUS**
Married 46.2%
Unmarried 53.8%

Percentage married to other service members: **6.6%**

Women married to other service members: **9.1%**

Men married to other service members: **2.0%**

■ **CHILDREN**
Have children 42.7%
Have no children 57.3%

Both parents in the military: **7,300**

Single parent: **29,000**

■ 19.6% are women, more than 5% percentage points higher than those on active duty

■ Just 26% of reservists are minorities, substantially lower than the active-duty Navy. Blacks comprise 14% of the reserve

■ 63% of Naval Reserve members are married, but only 2% are married to another service member

■ 45% have children. The average age at which naval reservists have their first child is 29

The **AIR FORCE** has the highest percentage of married members. On average, Air Force members are the oldest when their first child is born: 27

■ **MARITAL STATUS**
Married 59.9%
Unmarried 40.1%

Percentage married to other service members: **16.1%**

Women married to other service members: **24.9%**

Men married to other service members: **5.9%**

■ **CHILDREN**
Have children 47.7%
Have no children 52.3%

Both parents in the military: **12,500**

Single parent: **17,500**

■ The Air Force Reserve and Air National Guard have the highest average ages in the military. More than one-third are older than 40

■ The air reserves have the fewest minorities. 80% of the Air National Guard is white

■ The Air Force Reserve and Air National Guard have the highest marriage rates, 66% and 62%, respectively

■ Half of all Air Force Reserve and Air National Guard members have children

---

Among the military, **MARINES** are least likely to be married or have children. Women in the Marines are most likely to be married to another service member

■ **MARITAL STATUS**

Married 42.9%
Unmarried 57.1%

Percentage married to other service members: **8.7%**

Women married to other service members: **26.3%**

Men married to other service members: **2.2%**

■ **CHILDREN**

Have children 31.5%
Have no children 68.5%

Both parents in the military: **2,200**

Single parent: **5,500**

■ The Marine Corps has the youngest reserve force. Almost two-thirds of its members are younger than 25. About 6% are older than 40

■ Less than 5% of Marine reservists are women; about one-third are minorities

■ Like active-duty Marines, comparatively few reservists are married, only 30%

■ Marine reservists are the least likely to have children. Only 17% are parents, and the average age at which they have children is 26

---

ation, is now part of the Department of Homeland Security. During wartime, the Coast Guard can be assigned to the U.S. Navy.

Source: Department of Defense   TIME Graphic

Oasis in the City

Sweltering Parisians
seek relief from the sun
in the public fountains
at the Trocadero
Gardens on Aug. 8.
This would have been
a lovely scene—if it
didn't reflect a crisis.
A summer heat wave
that scorched nations
across Europe was
blamed for some 19,000
deaths, almost 15,000
in France alone. The
time-honored August
exodus of French
vacationers from the
nation's largest cities left
many older citizens
home alone with no
air-conditioning and
no care, while short-
staffed hospitals were
unable to aid many
victims of the heat.

**Photograph by
Norman Godwin—Corbis**

World

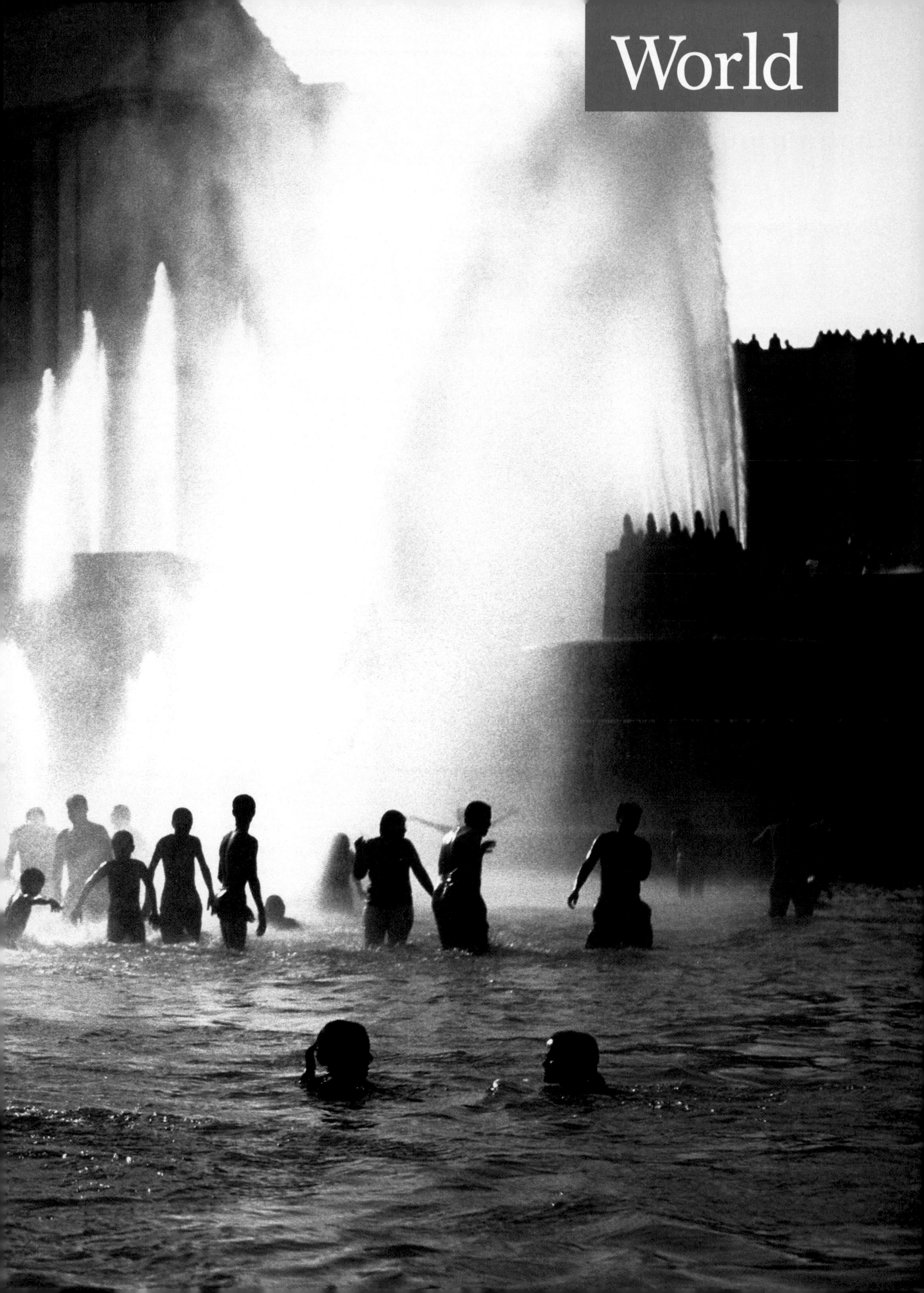

WAR ON TERROR: A BRIEFING

Suicide bombings in Saudi Arabia, Afghanistan, Morocco and Turkey were linked to al-Qaeda agents, suggesting the terror group is still active, though two of its key agents were apprehended in 2003. As of Dec. 15, Osama bin Laden and his No. 2 man were still at large

AT LARGE

OSAMA BIN LADEN: The first new videotape image of the al-Qaeda chief in almost two years was released on Sept. 10, 2003. In it, bin Laden and his chief deputy, Ayman al-Zawahiri, praise the 9/11 hijackers, and the latter says: "What you saw until now are only the first skirmishes; the true epic has not begun." As of Dec. 2003, the two are believed to be hiding in the border region between Afghanistan and Pakistan

MULLAH OMAR: Afghanistan's fugitive former head of state remained at large as of Dec. 15—and apparently he was in charge of a newly resurgent  Taliban, which staged more frequent and more highly organized attacks against coalition forces as the year went on

IN CUSTODY

ZACARIAS MOUSSAOUI: Legal wrangling clouded the case of the so-called "20th hijacker" in the 9/11 attacks. He may be tried by a military court

RICHARD REID: The Briton was sentenced to life in prison in January 2003 for his 2001 attempt to blow up an airliner with a shoe bomb

CAMP DELTA: The U.S. Supreme Court agreed in November to hear appeals from a group of 16 British, Australian and Kuwaiti nationals who are among the more than 600 alleged terrorists held at the U.S. naval base on Guantánamo Bay, Cuba. The suit argues that the U.S. has no legal authority to hold foreigners indefinitely without charge

NABBED

KHALID SHEIKH MOHAMMED: The mastermind of the 9/11 strikes was captured in Pakistan in March. He claims he killed U.S. reporter Daniel Pearl

HAMBALI: Al-Qaeda's top man in Asia was arrested by Thai authorities in August. He says he led the 2002 bombing of a Bali nightclub that killed 202 people

SAUDI ARABIA: On May 12, just hours before U.S. Secretary of State Colin Powell arrived in Riyadh, the capital, 15 operatives linked to al-Qaeda shot their way into three housing compounds and a business center and carried out four simultaneous suicide bombings. The attacks killed 34 people, including 10 Americans, a number of other foreign nationals, seven Saudis and nine of the terrorists

STRIKES IN 2003

TURKEY: On November 15, trucks pulled up in front of two of the largest and oldest synagogues in Istanbul and exploded. The blasts killed 23 people and wounded more than 300. DNA identification of the suicide bombers linked the deeds to an obscure al-Qaeda group. Five days later, as President Bush paid a state visit to England, another pair of coordinated car bombings in Istanbul hit the British Consulate and a British bank, killing 27 people and wounding hundreds more. A caller claiming to be from al-Qaeda took responsibility.

MOROCCO: Four days after the blasts in Riyadh in May, five simultaneous suicide bombings rocked Casablanca, above; twelve bombers and 33 bystanders were killed. Al-Qaeda is believed to have been responsible. Weeks later, a suicide bomber killed four German peace-keepers in Afghanistan. This attack was thought to be the work of Gulbuddin Hekmatyar, an Afghan warlord who is linked to Al Qaeda and the Taliban

DO FENCE ME IN

Ariel Sharon builds a massive barrier around Israel's territory. But in trying to keep suicide bombers at bay, is he also excluding peace?

THE WORDS THAT ISRAELI PRIME MINISTER ARIEL Sharon scrawled in a guest book during his July 29 visit to the White House were telling: "True friendship among allies can overcome every obstacle. No barrier can separate nations and leaders committed to peace, liberty and security." The barrier that Sharon had in mind was the series of stone walls, fortified trenches, electronic fences and razor wire that Israel began creating in the spring of 2003 around Jerusalem, through the middle of Bethlehem and eventually, across much of the occupied West Bank. The stated purpose of this structure was to deny suicide bombers access to Israel. Many Palestinians thought it was also meant to exert a stranglehold over their economy and unilaterally define the borders of a future

Palestinian state along lines that would leave in Arab hands just 45% of the territory set aside for them in previous agreements.

Just days before Sharon's White House visit, Bush had condemned the barrier (which Palestinians refer to as "a wall" and Israelis describe as "a fence"), saying at a White House meeting on July 25 with Palestinian Prime Minister Mahmoud Abbas that "it is very difficult to develop confidence between the Palestinians and Israel with a wall snaking through the West Bank." But during Sharon's visit, Bush carefully toned down his opposition to the edifice.

The "wall" or "fence" or "painfully apt metaphor for the state of the peace process" (take your pick) was only the latest setback for the U.S.-sponsored "road map to

MAY: Under heavy U.S. pressure, Yasser Arafat, who is tainted by his terrorist associations, agreed to name a Prime Minister for Palestine. His choice, Mahmoud Abbas, met with Ariel Sharon in Jerusalem in May. But a frustrated Abbas resigned in September

NOVEMBER: After Abbas resigned, Arafat named Ahmed Qurei, speaker of the Palestinian Parliament, as his replacement. In November a group of Israelis and Palestinians met in Geneva to sign a "virtual treaty," but neither Israel nor Palestine endorsed it

KEEP OUT! A Palestinian paints an anti-Israeli slogan on the security wall in Qalqilya, in the West Bank, on July 31. The wall is more than 26 ft. high

peace"—a plan calling for the Israelis to dismantle new settlements in the occupied territories, freeze construction in older outposts and take "all necessary steps to help normalize Palestinian life," while requiring the Palestinians to crack down on terror groups and confiscate all illegal weapons. The road map envisions Palestinian statehood by 2005, but even before the plan's formal unveiling at a June summit in Aqaba, Jordan, both sides seemed to be backing away from the plan.

Hopes had been high when Palestine's Abbas met with Sharon in May (in the first high-level Israeli-Palestinian talks in three years) and demanded that Israel release thousands of Palestinian prisoners and announce wholesale troop pullbacks from the West Bank. When Sharon refused, Abbas (who had been named Prime Minister by Palestinian Authority President Yasser Arafat in March, under heavy U.S. pressure) announced that he was powerless to disarm radical militant groups without starting a civil war. As if to underscore his impotence, two suicide bombings killed seven people in Jerusalem hours after the Sharon-Abbas meeting ended.

Some of the worst suicide terrorist attacks in Israel's history followed. Seven days after the Aqaba meeting, a bus attack in Jerusalem killed 17 people; a similar bombing killed 22 people. During this time, Abbas worked frantically to restrain militant groups without confronting them militarily. Israel retaliated on Aug. 21, assassinating senior Hamas leader Ismail Abu Shanab. Combined with a succession of fatal Israeli shootings of unarmed Palestinians at military checkpoints (including a 4-year-old boy on July 25), the killing of Shanab scotched the cease-fire. Abbas, who had never had the full support of Arafat, resigned in frustration early in September; Arafat named Palestinian parliament speaker Ahmed Qurei to succeed him. On Sept. 9, simultaneous suicide bombings at a café and an army base killed 15 Israelis, and two days later, Sharon's Cabinet voted to "remove" Arafat, without clarifying whether that meant deporting or killing him.

Three weeks later, another suicide bombing killed 21 people in a Haifa restaurant, and the next day, Oct. 5, Israel struck back with an air strike against Syria, which the Sharon government alleges is behind the militant group Islamic Jihad. Israelis somberly observed the beginning of the Day of Atonement, the holiest date on the Jewish calendar—and the 30th anniversary of 1973's October War—by bombing a neighboring Arab country and burying their own dead. The future looked grim for many Israelis, but promising for the nation's fence-building companies. ∎

AUGUST: A suicide bomber struck a bus returning from the Wailing Wall on the 19th, killing **17 people** and injuring close to **100.** After this event, the Israeli government launched a series of targeted assassinations, killing Hamas leader Ismail Abu Shanab

SEPTEMBER: On the 9th, the seaside town of Haifa was rocked by a pair of simultaneous bombings. Above, a café on Maxim Beach was struck by a female suicide bomber; a dead victim sits slumped in a chair. After these attacks, Sharon vowed to "remove" Arafat

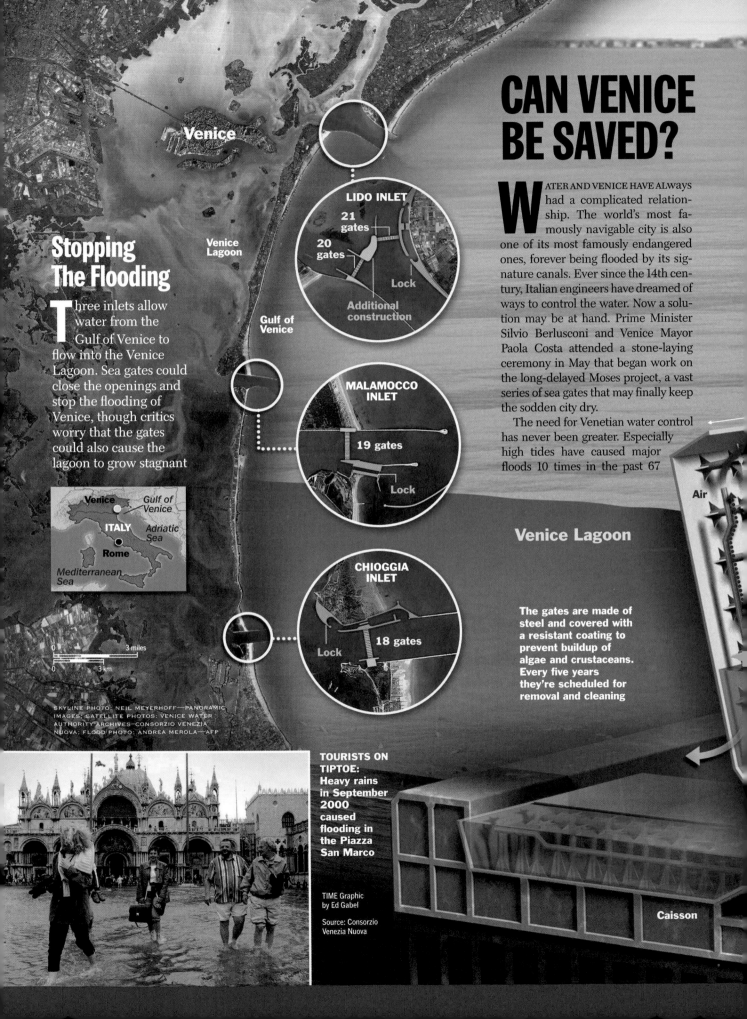

CAN VENICE BE SAVED?

Venice

LIDO INLET

21 gates

20 gates

Lock

Additional construction

Venice Lagoon

Gulf of Venice

Stopping The Flooding

Three inlets allow water from the Gulf of Venice to flow into the Venice Lagoon. Sea gates could close the openings and stop the flooding of Venice, though critics worry that the gates could also cause the lagoon to grow stagnant

Venice
Gulf of Venice

ITALY

Adriatic Sea

Rome

Mediterranean Sea

0 ___ 3 miles
0 ___ 3 km

MALAMOCCO INLET

19 gates

Lock

CHIOGGIA INLET

Lock   18 gates

W ATER AND VENICE HAVE ALWAYS had a complicated relationship. The world's most famously navigable city is also one of its most famously endangered ones, forever being flooded by its signature canals. Ever since the 14th century, Italian engineers have dreamed of ways to control the water. Now a solution may be at hand. Prime Minister Silvio Berlusconi and Venice Mayor Paola Costa attended a stone-laying ceremony in May that began work on the long-delayed Moses project, a vast series of sea gates that may finally keep the sodden city dry.

The need for Venetian water control has never been greater. Especially high tides have caused major floods 10 times in the past 67

Venice Lagoon

Air

The gates are made of steel and covered with a resistant coating to prevent buildup of algae and crustaceans. Every five years they're scheduled for removal and cleaning

SKYLINE PHOTO: NEIL MEYERHOFF—PANORAMIC IMAGES; SATELLITE PHOTOS: VENICE WATER AUTHORITY ARCHIVES—CONSORZIO VENEZIA NUOVA; FLOOD PHOTO: ANDREA MEROLA—AFP

TOURISTS ON TIPTOE: Heavy rains in September 2000 caused flooding in the Piazza San Marco

TIME Graphic by Ed Gabel

Source: Consorzio Venezia Nuova

Caisson

years alone, most disastrously in 1966, when water in parts of the city climbed to more than 6 ft. above sea level and swamped historic museums. Compression of the sediment under the city, acting in tandem with globally rising sea levels, frequently causes smaller floods, shutting down businesses and making sidewalks and squares impassable.

The source of the problem is geography. Venice is primarily a small cluster of interlocked islands set in the northern end of a 207-sq.-mi. lagoon. A long ridge of land separates the lagoon from the far larger Gulf of Venice, except at three major inlets. These openings allow high gulf tides to become high Venetian tides, with the water climbing high enough to swamp the city's seawalls.

In 1984 a commission composed of Italy's 50 largest engineering and construction firms was formed to find a way to control the water flow through the inlets, and Moses is it. Moses, an acronym for the plan's technical name as well

as a lyrical reference to the parting of the Red Sea, calls for 78 hollow sea gates—each up to 16 ft. thick, 65 ft. wide and 90 ft. long—to be hinged to foundations, or caissons, in the seabed and to lie flat there. The gates would usually be filled with water, but when tides rise to a height of 43 in. or more above sea level, compressed air would pump the water out. The free end of the gates would then float upward, breaking the surface after about 30 minutes and sealing off the inlets. Sea locks would permit ships to pass while the gates are up.

The project—which would take as long as 10 years and cost at least $2.7 billion—could still run into obstacles, especially given the fickle nature of Italian politics. An environmental-impact review now under way could slow or even scuttle construction. Even so, this is the closest Venice has come to a final solution to its water problems in 700 years. By local bureaucratic standards, that's not bad. ∎

gate: 65 ft. (20 m)

60 to 90 ft. (18 to 28 m)

Rising Waters

Venice has been slowly sinking because of rising sea levels and sediment compression

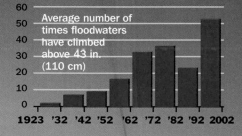

Average number of times floodwaters have climbed above 43 in. (110 cm)

1923 '32 '42 '52 '62 '72 '82 '92 2002

Gulf of Venice

Compressed air

How the Gates Would Work

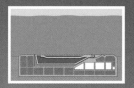

The 78 hollow sea gates are filled with water most of the time and remain out of sight in a foundation or caisson

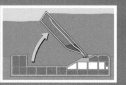

During especially high tides, compressed air flushes out the seawater. Within 30 min. the gates rise to the surface and block the inlets

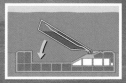

When the danger passes, water is admitted back into the gates, causing them to sink within 15 min.

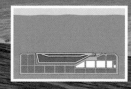

The gates remain on the sea floor until they're needed, which will happen whenever the tides climb to a height of 43 in. (110 cm)

An End to the Madness—For Now

Dictator Charles Taylor is finally ousted. Will he take the chaos with him?

GANG RULE: Above, forces loyal to Charles Taylor roll through the city of Ganta in June. Right, Taylor waves farewell as he embarks into exile in August

WE ARE HEARING THE NEWS every day that they are coming, they are coming," said a resident of a Liberian refugee camp in July about the rumored imminent arrival of U.S. troops, "but we keep dying." Founded more than 150 years ago by freed American slaves, Liberia has descended over the past 14 years into a nightmare of madness, bloodletting and power struggles among competing rebel groups. The country's stalemated civil war, in which most of the casualties have been civilians and whose warriors include heavily armed small children high on drugs, has been marked by rape, torture and cannibalism. Ringmaster of this carnival of madness was a dictator indicted by a U.N.-backed war crimes court, President Charles Taylor.

❝ The war is over … History will be kind to me. I have accepted this role as the sacrificial lamb. ❞ —CHARLES TAYLOR

As the violence reached a high-water mark in 2003 and rebel forces made new gains against Taylor's government, neighboring African countries (motivated in part by fears that Liberia's instability would slip across the border) began to abandon him, and an international consensus emerged that Liberia's President since 1997 would have to go. Seeming to accept his fate, Taylor declared in June that he would step down. But he soon waffled on his offer, putting conditions on it and pushing back the date of his departure. It quickly became clear that the opinion of the outside world was largely meaningless in Liberia, absent a peacekeeping force to back it up.

In July, President George W. Bush declared that sending American troops to Liberia as part of a larger multinational force might be an option. But he attached a condition of his own: U.S. troops would not land in Liberia until Taylor had resigned and left the country.

In the weeks that followed, Taylor played for time and the Pentagon ordered three U.S. warships to lie at anchor just off the coast of Liberia but not to land troops. The pressure on the U.S. was ratcheted up several notches in July and August, when Liberian refugees began dumping the bodies of murdered family members at the gates of the U.S. embassy in Monrovia, hoping to shock into action the nation that Liberians look upon as a kind of godfather to their own. When a small team of U.S. troops came ashore in late July to conduct a preliminary reconnaissance, they were mobbed by Liberian civilians pleading for help.

In the end, it was action by Liberians themselves that brought matters to a head. A new offensive by rebel groups in the last two weeks of July convinced Taylor that he was safer out of Liberia than in. On Aug. 1, the U.N. Security Council voted to back a multinational peacekeeping force for Liberia, and the first troops (from neighboring Nigeria) arrived three days later. Taylor at last resigned; he left the country on Aug. 11, accepting Nigeria's offer of asylum. Three days later, a contingent of 225 U.S. troops arrived to assist Nigerian peacekeepers, pending the arrival of more multinational troops. Most of the American force left 10 days later, and U.S. warships departed Liberian waters at the end of September.

On Oct. 14, Gyude Bryant, a compromise candidate chosen by the nation's two main rebel groups and Taylor's own party, was sworn in as the two-year interim leader of Liberia's new government. "The war is over, my people," he said at the ceremony. "Never again." Taylor, who is estimated to have stolen $100 million during his time in office and is known to have left Liberia with at least $3 million in cash, now says, "History will be kind to me. I have accepted this role as the sacrificial lamb." *Baaah.* ∎

An Outlaw State Rattles Its Cage

The defiant Stalinist regime says it has a big stick. How long will it walk softly?

GONG YIDONG—AP/WIDE WORLD

SO, THERE! Above, some **1 million North Koreans** hail their defiance of the global nuclear treaty. Right, President Kim Jong Il meets Russian diplomats in January

KOREA NEWS SERVICE—AP/WIDE WORLD

NORTH KOREA BEGAN 2003 WITH A FIGURATIVE BANG that seemed to foreshadow more literal explosions to come. On the last day of 2002, the Hermit Kingdom expelled United Nations weapons inspectors who were responsible for monitoring nuclear facilities that had been deactivated, in a deal with the U.S., since 1994. Ten days after the inspectors were booted from the country, North Korea formally withdrew from the Nuclear Nonproliferation Treaty, which it had signed in 1985, becoming the first signatory nation in the history of the treaty to repudiate it. Cowed citizens saluted the act with a parade.

Weeks later, on Feb. 6, North Korea publicly acknowledged for the first time that it had restarted its nuclear-reactor facilities and was using the atomic plants to produce weapons-grade plutonium. Later in February, U.S. intelligence agencies confirmed that this was the case. The saber rattling continued when North Korea fired an anti-ship missile into the Pacific Ocean the day before the inauguration of South Korean President Roh Moo-hyun.

In spite of such provocations, President Bush described himself as "confident" that a resolution could be achieved without military action, and Washington's rhetoric remained low-key throughout the year. The White House instead emphasized quiet regional diplomacy to bring North Korea to the negotiating table.

The approach worked—especially after the Bush Administration convinced China to shut down a vital oil pipeline to North Korea in March. Preliminary talks began in Beijing in April, around the time Pyongyang blithely declared it had completed building several nuclear devices and would test, sell or use them, depending on the progress of the negotiations. (Although Western intelligence analysts take North Korea's nuclear potential seriously, most were skeptical that the country's program had advanced that far.) By August, the talks had expanded to include Russia, Japan and South Korea as well as the U.S. and China, but they ended abruptly when North Korea demanded immediate concessions—in the form of food, money and oil, in addition to a treaty guaranteeing that the U.S. would never attack North Korea—prior to any further discussion.

President Bush responded in early October by offering a verbal assurance that the U.S. would not invade North Korea, although he refused to sign a binding treaty to that effect. Pyongyang dismissed this as "a laughing matter." But by the end of the month, North Korea had agreed to return to the talks. Where they will lead, no one can be certain. But at least for the moment, all sides seemed to agree with Winston Churchill's famous 1954 comment about another set of stalemated negotiations with North Korea: "To jaw-jaw is better than to war-war." ■

■ North Korea becomes the first signatory to ditch the Nuclear Nonproliferation Treaty ■

■ PROFILE

Taking Down an Oligarch

In Russia's first years as a market economy, crooks and businessmen were one and the same. But Mikhail Khodorkovsky, 40, the richest man in Russia, has been a one-man reform movement. His Yukos Oil Co. enjoys a reputation among foreign investors as perhaps the most Western-like company in Russia. It has a cluster of Americans on its board and among top management, it uses U.S. accounting standards,

KHODORKOVSKY: On the hot seat

and it was the first Russian company to detail its precise ownership structure. But on Oct. 27, Khodorkovsky was arrested on tax evasion and other charges, after months of Kremlin intimidation. Prosecutors froze his 44% stake in Yukos, the world's fourth largest oil company and the source of Khodorkovsky's wealth, estimated in 2002 at $8 billion. Khodorkovsky denies any wrongdoing, and his lawyers say the charges are purely political. Many in Russia view the arrest as the centerpiece of a power struggle between "the Siloviki," as President Vladimir Putin's coterie of security officials and bureaucrats is known, and "the Family," the billionaire oligarchs and top officials who thrived during the wild days of privatization under former President Boris Yeltsin.

SCOTLAND: After 15 years, Gadaffi said he will compensate victims' families

Gaddafi Accepts the Blame

Libyan leader Muammar Gaddafi agreed in August to pay as much as $5 million to relatives of each of the 270 victims of Pan Am Flight 103, downed over Lockerbie, Scotland, in 1988. He also sent a statement to the U.N. Security Council renouncing terrorism and accepted blame for the actions of a Libyan spy found guilty of blowing up the craft. A U.S.-backed agreement calls on the U.N. to permanently lift sanctions on Libya, which were suspended in 1999 after Gaddafi handed over two suspects.

A Setback in Serbia

Prime Minister Zoran Djindjic brought real reform to Serbia, engineering the ouster of dictator Slobodan Milosevic. On March 12, Djindjic, 50, was shot down by gunmen in Belgrade. Police rounded up some 2,000 people suspected of ties to an underworld group led by a Milosevic associate that opposes Djindjic. Forty-four people charged with conspiring in the murder went on trial late in December.

CHINA: Jiang and Hu grip and grin

China Shuffles the Deck

As China retreats ever farther from the revolutionary heritage of Mao Zedong, President Jiang Zemin, 77, left, stepped aside on March 15 in favor of a hand-picked successor, Hu Jintao, 60. Jiang maintained his hold over the nation's military, however, ensuring that his voice would be heard in Beijing circles. In July, the leadership was rocked when 500,000 protesters took to the streets of Hong Kong to protest new antisubversion laws that placed curbs on individual rights.

SERBIA: Mourning a slain leader

Images

Rattling China
An earthquake shook the remote Xinjiang region of western China on Feb. 24, killing at least 257 people, injuring more than 1,000 and flattening homes and schools. The most severe quake to strike Xinjiang in five decades measured 6.8 on the Richter scale; the worst damage centered on the ancient Silk Road oasis of Kashgar. Left, a newly homeless villager camps out in near freezing cold.

Russian Navy Hits Bottom

Only three years after the Russian nuclear sub *Kursk* sank, killing 118, another rust bucket, the *K-159*, went down in the Barents Sea in September as it was being towed to a navy scrap yard. Although its

RUSSIA: The *K-159* was built in 1963

nuclear reactors had not fired up in 15 years, *K-159* was carrying 1,760 lbs. of spent nuclear fuel. Russian officials said they would raise the ship—but didn't say when. The good news: monitors have so far found no radioactive leakage.

Revolt in Indonesia

The Indonesian military launched a massive campaign against the separatist Free Aceh Movement in May, after new peace talks with the group collapsed. The fiercely nationalistic people of the northern Sumatra province have long resented what they call an illegitimate occupation by Indonesia. In 27 years of fighting, some 12,000 people have lost their lives.

Iran: Building a Bomb?

Under fire for its suspected pursuit of nuclear weapons, Iran came clean in response to questions from the International Atomic Energy Agency (IAEA) in the fall. The country admitted that it had produced enriched uranium at the Kalay-e electric plant outside Tehran, a violation of its agreements with the IAEA. The revelation was part of a series of revealing disclosures Tehran made in an attempt to avoid threatened international sanctions for its suspected nuclear activities.

ACEH: Villagers wait to receive rations from soldiers of the Indonesian military

It's a Bad Thing

Life wasn't so gracious for doyen of good living Martha Stewart in 2003. At right, she is swept up in a media maelstrom after she pleaded not guilty to charges of illegal securities trading at the U.S. District Court in New York City on June 4. Stewart's celebrity made her the poster girl for corporate malfeasance, though her alleged misdeeds are small potatoes alongside those of executives involved with the Enron, Worldcom and Adelphia scandals of 2002. They may be responsible for billions of dollars lost to tens of thousands of individual investors and for draining the retirement accounts of thousands of longtime workers. Meanwhile, charges of corruption rocked the mutual-funds industry. Such funds have long been marketed as the safest investment for middle-class Americans.

Business

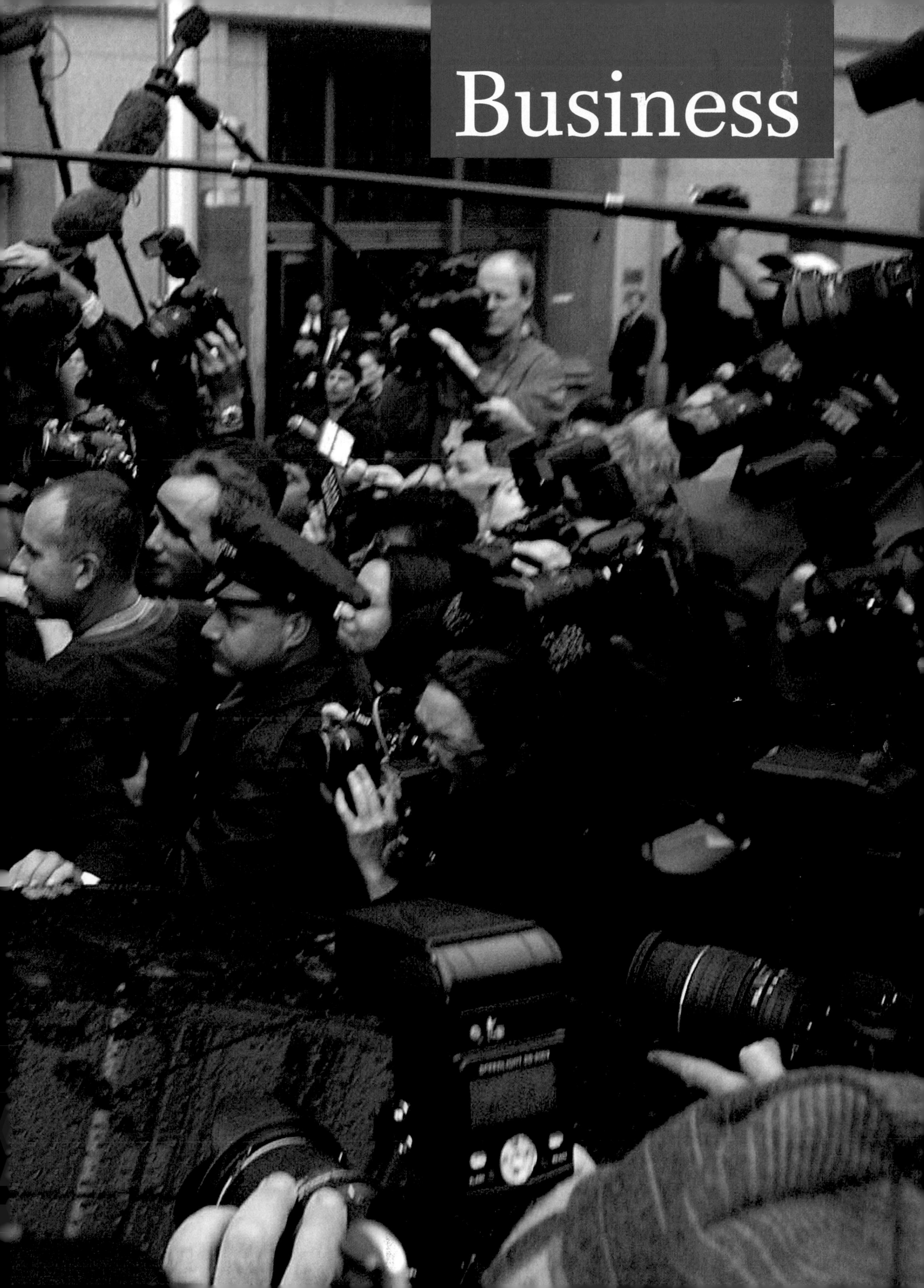

RIP

MIX

BURN

WHEN PIRATES PAY UP

While the music industry cracks down on digital file-swappers with a raft of lawsuits, a computer firm makes buying music online cool

AS DIGITAL BOOTLEGGING (OR, IF YOU prefer, software piracy) continues to change the way many people obtain music, the numbers are ugly enough to scare a gangsta rapper: CD shipments were down 9% for 2002, on top of a 6% decline in 2001. An estimated 60 million Americans use the Internet file-sharing networks that contain digitally bootlegged music. They're swapping some 400,000 to 600,000 files (mostly songs and movies) every day. Sales of MP3 players rose 56%

in 2001-02, and while Americans did purchase 680 million albums in 2002, they also bought 1.7 billion blank CDs—up 40% from the year before. The clear implication: more and more users are downloading free music and burning it onto blank CDs. It's information-superhighway robbery.

If 2002 was the year that the recording industry fell off a digital cliff, 2003 was the

THIEF? Bob Barnes, 50, snags hard-to-find European artists on the Internet. He was subpoenaed by the record industry in July

GARY KAZANJIAN—AP/WIDE WORLD

year when it finally decided to take action. But neither of the approaches chosen—the bad-cop route of filing lawsuits against downloaders, the good-cop route of inventing superior pay-to-play websites—proved wholly successful. Salvation eventually arrived from outside the music industry, courtesy of a computer maker.

After shutting down Napster, the most prominent of the file-sharing networks, in 2002, the industry turned its attention to the customers of these services. On Sept. 8, the Recording Industry Association of America began filing waves of lawsuits, litigating against hundreds of individuals—college students, lawyers, bus drivers and in one case a 12-year-old girl. At $150,000 per pirated song, some of these actions were asking for damages of more than $1 billion. It was a strong stand, but it only cemented the public's view that the recording industry was far more enamored of money than music.

Meanwhile, record labels set out to offer legitimate alternatives for people who were willing to pay to download music. This meant abandoning the fractious, abortive efforts of the past five years, in which most label websites alienated consumers with limited selection, clunky interfaces, record-store prices and restrictions seemingly designed to please copyright lawyers and annoy customers. But none of the revised pay websites caught on with downloaders.

Enter a third party: Steve Jobs of Apple Computer. In April, Jobs leveraged the success of the company's already white-hot iPod MP3 player by launching the iTunes Music Store—a legal online music service that eliminated monthly fees and let people burn the songs they purchased onto an unlimited number of CDs. The service carried the blessing of the record labels, from which Apple had licensed rights to hundreds of thousands of songs. In the first 18 hours after the Music Store went live on April 28, buyers paid for an estimated 275,000 songs at 99¢ a track, or about $10 an album.

RICHARD DREW—AP/WIDE WORLD

LEGAL: Rapper Ludacris accesses his music on the new Napster 2.0 pay service, which debuted in the fall of 2003

66 Who wants to be put in jail because you downloaded Justin Timberlake's newest song? 99

By September, Apple had sold more than 10 million songs, outpacing its rosiest predictions. But licensing and service costs were high. As Jobs admitted, "It's not a way to make a lot of money." It did turn out, however, to be a great way to sell high-profit-margin iPods; sales almost quadrupled in the quarters before and after the iTunes launch. In mid-October, Apple unveiled a new version of iTunes that was compatible with computers running Microsoft Windows, putting it within reach of the 97% of computer users not running the Macintosh operating system.

The success of Apple's site proved that consumers were willing to pay for a fairly priced, user-friendly downloading service rather than continue to purloin free music illegally. As one put it, "Who wants to be put in jail or pay some huge fine because you downloaded Justin Timberlake's newest song? It's just too big of a risk." And with that, one more software pirate hung up his eye patch. ∎

■ PAY OR SWAP? THE CHOICES

Ask high school students if they use the most common free file-swapping service, Kazaa, and the answer is a resounding "duh."

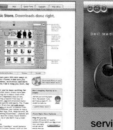

stepped into the breach. Dell Computer, the nation's No. 1 PC seller, launched a site of its own, right, while Apple's iTunes

The recording industry hasn't come up with workable websites that combine ease of use with a price that seems fair. Sites where users can pay to download files legally, like the Rhapsody system, left, which charges $10 a month for a membership, attracted few customers. As the recording industry floundered, computer makers service, center, quickly became the new standard. And guess what's back? In the fall a reworked (and legal) version of the original swapping service, Napster, was launched. The new guilt-free site offered consumers a choice between a monthly subscription plan or a pay-per-song download fee—a combination that was a first for the industry. The revolution continues...

A NEW PEAK FOR GEEK CHIC

Cell-phone cameras? Key-ring MP3 players? *Come Together* was the mantra as the year's coolest high-tech toys sprouted extra powers, even as they continued to shrink in size

DISPOSABLE DIGITALS
This single-use digital camera costs **$10.99** and lets you delete shots that don't pan out

OLYMPUS ZOOM
Digital cameras like this C-740 now offer 10X optical zoom lenses for $499—a real upgrade

KODAK ZOOM
Kodak's EasyShare DX6490 builds in the zoom feature, with 4-megapixel resolution

TINY DIGITAL CAMERAS
For $200 to $500, they offer loads of features and sharp quality in a minuscule package

CELL-PHONE CAMERAS
The year's biggest craze in electronics was the cell-phone camera; estimates suggest between 3 and 6 million were sold in '03. Though the pictures they took were often grainy or blurry, the novelty value won out. But what to do with all those snapshots? Phone-cam blogs began popping up on the Web, offering virtual galleries of life in a digital age

HARISH TYAGI—EPA/WIDE WORLD

ASIMO THE ROBOT
Was it only a few years ago that Sony wowed us with its robot dog? Not to be outdone, rival Honda now offers Asimo, whose name pays homage to the author of the sci-fi classic *I, Robot,* Isaac Asimov. The metal man (he's a prototype; there are no retail versions yet) served as an envoy to Japanese Prime Minister Junichiro Koizumi at a state dinner in the Czech Republic, where Asimo placed a bouquet of flowers by the bust of writer Karel Capek, who coined the term robot in his 1921 play, *R.U.R.*

CARGOMAXX
This $299 battery-powered wheelbarrow from Country Home Products lets you lug up to 400 lbs. of stuff at speeds up to 3 m.p.h. Grab the handles to balance it

AQUOS WIRELESS TV
Your phone is cordless ... so why not ditch the ugly cords around your TV? Sharp's $1,800 set will allow peripheral devices like DVD players and cable boxes to connect via a transmitter, freeing you to move the TV around the house

TED THAI FOR TIME

LIGHTTRO BULBS
These snazzy light sources from Color Kinetics are a lot of fun. Each bulb has 11 LED lights controlled by a PC circuit board that directs a variety of effects—including strobe—and a rotating spectrum of colors

USB KEY RINGS
These tiny devices plug directly into your USB port for easy up- and downloading. Always fun and trendy, they're getting more useful all the time. Two 2003 key rings from Philips show their potential. The MP3 key ring comes in 64-MB and 128-MB sizes, just right for a short music playlist. The 1.3-megapixel camera, above, weighs in at only 1.2 oz. Price: $99 to $149

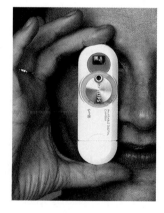

MINIATURE VIDEO RECORDERS
A new flock of tiny video recorders hit the U.S. market late in '03. To save programs, you plug the recorder directly into your TV, cable box or TiVo player; the picture is surprisingly good. Panasonic's SV-AV30 (above, $400), combines a video recorder with a mini-camcorder, still camera and MP3 player, but its memory is meager

INADA MASSAGE CHAIR
The D.1 chair uses a system of computer-controlled rollers that firmly press into your back while inflatable air bags squeeze tension from your extremities. You'll need to be relaxed when you see the price tag: $4,900

ORKA OVEN MITT
This pricey ($30) grabber from iSi North America is made of silicone. Heat- and flame-resistant up to 500°F, the stainproof glove allows you to pluck hard-boiled eggs right out of boiling water—but, ironically, it's a bit stiff for pulling pans from the oven

Big Pay, Big Trouble at the Big Board

How much is too much? Ask the former boss of the New York Stock Exchange

WHO, ME? Grasso first defended his outsize payout, then attempted to deter critics by refusing some of it. In the end, he left his post

HERE'S A HORATIO ALGER STORY WITH A MODERN TWIST. A working-class kid from Queens joins a big outfit as a lad and spends his entire career there, eventually rising to the top. In the last chapter, he triumphs in a moment of grave crisis, adding fame to fortune. The latter-day Alger? Dick Grasso, who joined the N.Y.S.E. in 1968 as an $80-a-week clerk, rose to run it and, as its chairman and CEO, radiated calm competence in the days after Sept. 11, 2001. Steadying jittery financial markets, Grasso, 57, had traders back on the floor of the exchange within a week of the terrorist attacks, while much of the Lower Manhattan neighborhood outside the N.Y.S.E.'s Greco-Roman façade was deserted and still swathed in the dust of Ground Zero.

Too bad Grasso's story didn't end there. In May 2003, reports surfaced that his 2002 compensation package had totaled more than $10 million. Many critics found this hard to digest, especially since Grasso had recently been pushing for stricter rules and more transparency for N.Y.S.E. members. But surprise turned to outrage when further revelations pegged Grasso's 2002 pay package at $12 mil-

lion and his 2001 compensation at more than $20 million. And outrage turned to pure rage when the exchange disclosed in August that Grasso was planning by the end of 2003 to cash out a package of deferred compensation and retirement benefits worth more than $140 million.

Grasso tried to quell critics by disclosing a further $48 million the N.Y.S.E.'s board of directors had agreed to pay him by 2007 and and said he would forgo it. But it was too little, too late. A chorus of critics cited the inherent conflict of interest that arises when a stunningly generous compensation package for a senior executive is approved by a board of directors appointed by him. In Grasso's case, the conflict was worsened by the fact that the exchange helps regulate its member firms, and that its board consisted largely of executives from the companies Grasso was supposedly charged with policing.

By mid-September, state treasurers, major pension-fund managers and Democratic presidential contenders were calling for Grasso to quit. On Sept. 17, in an impromptu board meeting held by telephone after trading had ended for the day, Grasso offered to step down. The board agreed, and the first N.Y.S.E. president ever to come up through the ranks of the organization was gone. Within two weeks, the board had settled on former Citigroup CEO John Reed as Grasso's interim replacement. Reed's compensation package? One dollar a year. ∎

❝ No P.R. can help Grasso ... There is no answer to pure greed. ❞ —P.R. VETERAN JACK O'DWYER

On the Streets, It's Back to the Future

What exactly are these vehicles? We have no idea—but we're going in style

SURF BUGGY: What has mondo headroom, an appealing homeliness with odd-size doors and three-tone trim? The 1946 woody—and the 2003 Honda Element

RAKISH PICKUP: The luxurious half-SUV, half-pickup Caddy Escalade EXT hauls people, hauls cargo and hauls butt. The 1978 Subaru Brat was also an SUV-car-pickup with four-wheel drive

HONDA; RON KIMBALL (WOODY); CADILLAC; NISSAN; DAIMLER CHRYSLER; SCOUT CONNECTION (HARVESTER)

"THIS IS NOT YOUR FATHER'S OLDSMOBILE." THAT GUTSY advertising slogan, which came right out and admitted that a longtime GM brand was suffering from a perception problem, was eventually canned. The car company decided it was only reinforcing the line's image problems, not resolving them. A few years later, the Oldsmobile line itself—one of the great American car marques, bearing the name of automotive genius Ransom Olds—was also consigned to history's junkyard.

But now ... well, if this isn't exactly your father's car, at the least there's a family resemblance. Automakers are crafting new models that are high-tech updates of familiar old cars. Sometimes the resulting amalgam simply eludes the usual classifications. Take a look at the Cadil-

lac Escalade EXT at the top right. Is it a car? A truck? A wagon? A van? An SUV? The answer: all of the above. Car companies are sewing together design elements and features from wildly different vehicles to create "crossovers," such as a minivan combined with a wagon and an SUV, as in the Chrysler Pacifica, below left.

Who would have dreamed that we'd live to see the day when the goofy AMC Gremlin got a makeover? Well, who would have dreamed that snooty Cadillac would score its commercials to a shrieking Led Zeppelin rave-up—albeit one that is 30 years old—and make them work? It's a brand-new, grand-old world out there on the streets, and here are four examples of the hybrid designs that car designers are cooking up in their crucibles. ■

WAGONS HO! Chrysler called its 2004 Pacifica with three-row seating for six a "sports tourer." We see a tall wagon—not unlike the imposing International Harvester Travelall from 1974. Buyers didn't see the point; early sales figures were disappointing

HIGH-STYLE HATCHBACK: Nissan says its Murano is an "urban SUV." Read: a jaunty, high-bodied hatchback that doesn't belong off road. Wait—couldn't that describe the wild 1974 AMC Gremlin?

CROWING: NBC's Robert Wright, second from right, celebrates the Vivendi buyout

■ PROFILE

Adios to the Love Bug

What a journey! The Volkswagen Beetle was conceived under one of history's greatest monsters, but it became perhaps the most widely beloved vehicle ever created, a symbol of the groovy '60s and the "Love Bug" of a series of Disney movies. In October a final run of 3,000 original-version Beetles rolled off the assembly line in a Puebla, Mexico, plant. The facility will continue to make the popular

Volkswagen de México
Último Sedán del Mundo
30 de Julio 2003

KAPUT: The VW Beetle bows out

modern version of the compact classic, but the Bug is kaput.

Adolf Hitler asked auto wizard Ferdinand Porsche to create an inexpensive "People's Car" in the 1930s. The first prototype was built in 1934, but World War II delayed the rollout of the affordable, trustworthy vehicle. The Beetle became the most widely produced car in automotive history; the last one off the line in Mexico, where the *"Vocho"* is widely used as a taxicab, was No. 21,529,464. The Bug was introduced to America in 1949; U.S. production of the car was halted in 1977, when it no longer met emissions standards. The "last edition" Bugs were earmarked for collectors and fitted out with whitewall tires and a CD player.

NBC Bulks Up on Vivendi

General Electric is the model of a modern major conglomerate, but even the big company isn't immune to a bad economy. Many of its divisions—plastics, power turbines, insurance—faltered in 2003; by fall the stock had been halved from its high of $60 in 2000. One exception: the NBC network, whose profits surged 20% for the first half of the year. Feeling his oats, NBC boss Robert Wright decided to branch out. He bought troubled Vivendi, the onetime French water company that ex-CEO Jean-Marie Messier tried—and failed—to build into a media empire. The asking price: $14 billion. The prize: the

Universal movie and TV studios, Universal's theme parks and cable networks including USA and Sci Fi. The move aligned NBC with the other major TV networks, all of which are affiliated with Hollywood studios.

Futuristic—and Obsolete

For 27 years the British-French supersonic airliner Concorde plied the skies above the Atlantic, whisking passengers from London to New York in 3.5 hours at twice the speed of sound—for prices up to $9,000. But operating costs for the needle-nosed craft were high, and the flagship of the Air France and British Airways fleets never

TOUCH DOWN: London Concorde fans gather to watch one of the jet's last landings

Images

Hear No Evil
Relief workers from Oxfam, a global relief agency, wear fiberglass heads of G-8 world leaders at a swimming pool near the World Trade Organization meeting in Cancún on Sept. 14. Opponents of global trade accuse wealthy nations of turning a deaf ear to the needs of poorer countries. Talks on the issue collapsed in Cancún, as the rift between rich and poor nations

NEW HUE: The brand new Andrew

returned the handsome profits it once promised. When a Concorde crashed just after take-off near Paris in July 2000, the entire fleet was grounded. Though the jets flew again, their days were numbered. On Oct. 24 the aircraft made its final flights, as three Concordes landed at London's Heathrow Airport in rapid succession.

The New Colors of Money

The U.S. Treasury says it plans to redesign all U.S. currency every seven to 10 years, in order to stay ahead of ever more sophisticated counterfeiters. First to roll out were the revamped $20 bills. The big surprise: they were the first multi-hued bills to nestle in U.S. wallets in 95 years. The new $20 features a peach color, which fades into green, supposedly making it more difficult for counterfeiters to match. On the back side, tiny numeral 20s in yellow float against the background, while TWENTY USA is printed in blue. On the front side, Andrew Jackson is freed from his oval vignette, allowing Old Hickory's long mane to flow into the border, and his shoulders are bulked up. The first bills went into circulation in late October; by the second week of November, Treasury officials said that they had begun to find counterfeit bills in circulation.

Big Media Under Fire

Federal Communications Commission chairman Michael Powell, son of Secretary of State Colin Powell, got a taste of friendly fire in 2003. When he issued new rules that would let broadcast giants like News Corp. and Viacom expand their media holdings in local markets, seven Republicans joined 28 Democrats in the Senate to endorse a rare "resolution of disapproval" to overturn the measures. In the House, defecting Republicans fueled a 40-to-25 committee vote to reverse part of the FCC's actions. Under pressure, Powell denied rumors he would leave his post.

POWELL: The FCC boss was dissed

Rock of Rages

The U.S. Constitution is well over 200 years old—and we're still fighting over the proper relationship between the church and the state. But Roy Moore, chief justice of the state of Alabama, was not troubled by uncertainty. A devout Christian (and perhaps even more devoted self-publicist), Moore orchestrated a daring nighttime art installation in 2001, when he placed a 5,280-lb. granite version of the Old Testament's Ten Commandments in the rotunda of the State Judicial Building in Montgomery, where he presided. A federal court ordered the monument's removal in August; Moore's eight fellow supreme court brethren agreed. But when the jurist refused to move "Roy's Rock," he was suspended from his duties. On Aug. 27, while scores of fundamentalist Christians knelt in prayer outside the building, workers rolled away the stone.

Photograph by Gary Tramontina— Getty Images

Society

HONOUR THY FATHER AND THY MOTHER
THOU SHALT NOT KILL
THOU SHALT NOT COMMIT ADULTERY
THOU SHALT NOT STEAL
THOU SHALT NOT BEAR FALSE WITNESS
THOU SHALT NOT COVET

A NEW DAY FOR GAYS?

A surprising Supreme Court ruling throws out antisodomy laws, while a furor over a gay bishop may divide the Anglican Church

TO CHART THE SEA CHANGE THAT HAS TAKEN PLACE IN the ongoing battle over the legal status of gay people in America, start at the top. Here are the words of the U.S. Supreme Court in April 1986, in the case of *Bowers v. Hardwick,* in which it upheld a Texas law making sodomy a crime: "Homosexual sodomy was a capital crime under Roman law … To hold that the act of homosexual sodomy is somehow protected as a fundamental right would be to cast aside millennia of moral teaching." Yet in June 2003, the court did cast such teachings aside, ruling in the case of *Lawrence v. Texas:* "The petitioners are entitled to respect for their private lives. The State cannot demean their existence or control their destiny by making their private sexual conduct a crime."

The court's turnaround was a milestone in a year that saw a series of victories for gay-rights activists in America and abroad. A few days after the surprising Supreme Court ruling, Wal-Mart, America's largest employer, announced it

UNDER FIRE: Once married, Bishop V. Gene Robinson has two grown children. He has lived with a male partner for 13 years

would expand its employee antidiscrimination protections to gays and lesbians. In the same month, Belgium and Canada became the second and third countries in the world (after the Netherlands) to legalize gay marriage. On Nov. 19, the Massachusetts Supreme Court ruled that gay marriage was legal, basing its decision on the state constitution, which guarantees equal rights for all. The decision promised to make gay marriage even more controversial; it may become a hot-button issue in the '04 elections.

But for every person who was cheered by these developments, there seemed to be another—or several others— who continued to find homosexual acts and gay marriage

profoundly immoral. Within days of the U.S. Supreme Court ruling, the U.S. Senate's G.O.P. leadership floated the idea of a constitutional amendment restricting the legal definition of marriage only to male-female unions and taking away the power of individual states to decide the issue locally. The move was led by Senator Rick Santorum of Pennsylvania, who earlier in the year publicly compared homosexual acts with adultery, bigamy and incest. But most state legislatures were already taking a hard line: Texas in 2003 became the 37th state to enact a law withholding legal recognition of same-sex unions formed in other states.

Even as U.S. antisodomy laws were being struck down, a furor erupted in Britain in May, when the Church of England appointed an openly gay theologian, Jeffrey John, as the Bishop of Reading. After meeting with Archbishop of Canterbury Rowan Williams, John declined to accept the appointment, citing concerns about church unity.

This flap was merely a foreshadowing of the firestorm of controversy that would engulf V. Gene Robinson, a priest of the Episcopal Church (the American affiliate of the Church of England), after he was elected bishop of New Hampshire. When his election was approved by a conference of Episcopal bishops in August, many Anglican parishes (not just in the U.S. and Britain but also around the world) declared themselves in open revolt. "With grief too deep for words, the bishops who stand before you must reject this action," said a spokesman for dissenting bishops.

A few days later, when the same conference of Episcopal bishops that had confirmed Robinson's election described the blessing of same-sex unions as "an acceptable practice within the church," the worldwide Anglican Church seemed to be reeling toward a historic schism.

Ironically, much of this weighty legal and religious wrangling seemed to occur in a different universe from the one in which gay retirement communities and even gay fraternities were becoming, if not commonplace, at least less rare, and TV shows like *Queer Eye for the Straight Guy* and *Boy Meets Boy* were bringing homosexuals further into the pop-culture mainstream.

But as gay-rights activists pointed out, the kinder, gentler media treatment of gays and even the new court rulings helped mask a more stubborn truth: despite all the talk of "domestic partners" and "civil unions," Massachusetts will be alone in allowing two people of the same sex to get legally married. And even if antisodomy laws are now void, in most states it remains perfectly legal to refuse employment or housing or even a seat at a restaurant to any person because of his or her sexual orientation. ■

To remedy the infringement of these constitutional rights, we ... declare the existing common law definition of marriage to be invalid to the extent that it refers to 'one man and one woman' —COURT OF APPEAL, ONTARIO

BIG DAY: Partners Heather Gass, right, and Lisa Lachance share a smile in Ottowa after a Canadian court cleared the way for legal same-sex marriage

In Vatican City, a Papacy at Twilight

An aged and ailing Pope John Paul II puts his final stamp on his Church

RED HEADS: On Oct. 21, John Paul gave the Cardinal's red hat to 30 bishops, who may soon be asked to elect his successor. Many people thought the Pope, who opposed the U.S.-led war in Iraq, might receive the Nobel Prize for peace in 2003, but he did not

J UNE, 1979. IN A TRIUMPHANT RE-turn to the land of his birth, Pope John Paul II, 59—formerly Karol Cardinal Wojtyla, Archbishop of Krakow—celebrates Mass before a crowd of millions. Elected in 1978, the Pope is a vital, commanding new figure on the world stage. The first non-Italian Pope in more than four centuries, he will soon offer critical support to Solidarity, the Polish labor movement, and will later be widely credited with helping bring about the end of the Soviet Empire.

In the years to come, this activist cleric will remake the papacy. The "pilgrim Pope" will travel to nations large and small to show his concern for his flock. He will reach out to Jews, Muslims and to other branches of Christianity in a major ecumenical campaign. With his enormous energy and charisma, he will make himself and his Roman Catholic Church church a formidable force in society.

But as TIME remarked in naming John Paul II its Man of the Year 1994, "When he talks, he expects his flock and the world to listen ... and they listen, not always liking what they hear." Indeed, the papacy of John Paul II is a bundle of contradictions. Though he is a modernizing force within the church, he is also a proponent of an old European version of Catholicism, a religion of pilgrimages and shrines, of miracle and relics, of rosaries and veneration of the Virgin Mary. He supports the radically conservative Opus Dei group within the church. He is a staunch opponent of birth control, homosexuality, the ordination of women, the inclusion of the laity in the liturgy and the sharing of power with his bishops. This pilgrim who preaches unity is also an autocrat who can sow division.

Oct. 21, 2003. In celebration of his 25th anniversary as Pope, John Paul II, now 83, presides over a week-long series of events at Vatican City. He beatifies Mother Teresa, the much admired nun of Calcutta's slums. He celebrates a Mass of thanksgiving in St. Peter's Square. And he ordains 30 bishops as Cardinals of the church.

Yet the man who presides over these events is merely a shadow of his younger self, and those who first encountered him in his prime are touched by his physical decline. This Karol Wojtyla suffers from symptoms of Parkinson's disease; at times he can barely speak, and then an associate handles that duty. He sits slumped in his chair, a haunting, living memento mori. As he places the red hat that symbolizes the office of Cardinal on the heads of a carefully chosen few, it is hard not to anticipate the day—seemingly coming soon—when these same Cardinals will gather to elect a new Pope. Since John Paul II has appointed 130 of the current 135-person College of Cardinals, it is a good chance that whoever they choose to succeed him will bear the stamp of this unforgettable Pontiff. ∎

∎ This pilgrim Pope who calls for unity is also an autocrat who can sow division ∎

Elizabeth Smart: Girl, Interrupted

After eight months of mystery, a missing Utah girl returns to her home

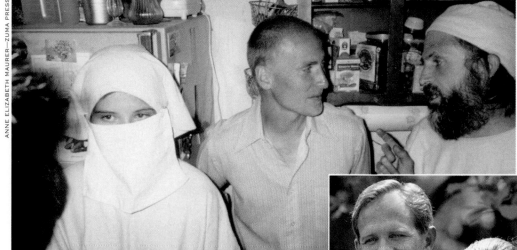

ANNE ELIZABETH MAURER—ZUMA PRESS

IN HIDING: Smart was caught on film at an August 2002 party in Salt Lake City. Brian D. Mitchell is at right. Below, Elizabeth joins parents Ed and Lois at the White House for the signing of the Amber Alert bill in April 2003

RON EDMONDS—AP/WIDE WORLD

THOU SAYETH," WAS THE CRYPTIC ANSWER THE YOUNG girl in the veil gave police in the small town of Sandy, Utah, on March 12, when they asked if her name was Elizabeth Smart. The officers had been alerted by passersby who had seen a recent episode of TV's *America's Most Wanted* and spotted the girl and two adults walking along the road wearing robes and crowns of flowers in their hair. Several thought the man leading the trio might be Brian David Mitchell, 49, wanted for questioning in the kidnapping, nine months earlier, of Smart, 15, from her home in nearby Salt Lake City.

The trembling young girl told the police her name was "Augustine" and denied again and again that she had been abducted, saying, "I know who you think I am. You guys think I'm that Elizabeth Smart girl who ran away." It was only after police separated the teenager from Mitchell and his wife Wanda Barzee and showed her a photo of Elizabeth Smart that she admitted her identity.

It was a suitably bizarre conclusion to a drama that began on the evening of June 5, 2002, when Mitchell, an eccentric with messianic pretensions who seven months earlier had worked as a handyman in the Smart house, allegedly cut a hole in a kitchen-window screen, then took Elizabeth at knifepoint from the bedroom she shared with her sister. Mitchell and Barzee are then believed to have led the girl up into the Wasatch Mountains, where for three months they camped in a maze of gullies and canyons only miles from the Smart home.

The Salt Lake City police chief now says that Elizabeth suffered a "strong psychological impact" that may have overwhelmed any impulse to escape. For his part, Mitchell claimed to be responding to a vision in which God commanded him to take seven additional wives. Mitchell,

> **❝ I know who you think I am. You think I'm that Elizabeth Smart girl who ran away. ❞**
>
> **—"AUGUSTINE," TO POLICE WHO FOUND HER**

Barzee and Smart lived openly for months on the streets of Salt Lake City, at one point camping out for weeks in the apartment of a benefactor just one block from police headquarters. They also wandered as far as San Diego.

At one point Mitchell was arrested in California, but he was quickly released. It wasn't until February 2003, when *America's Most Wanted* displayed a sketch of the man who called himself "Emmanuel," that the world began to close in on him. On March 12, two separate witnesses directed police to a group of strangely dressed vagabonds on State Street in Sandy, and Smart was rescued.

By November Smart had become a media sensation: her story was told in a book written by her parents, in a CBS movie and in a much sought first TV interview. "I think there's some things different about me," she told NBC's Katie Couric, "but I think I'm still pretty much the same person." Mitchell and Barzee await trial on charges of burglary, kidnapping and sexual assault. ∎

All the News That's Fixed to Print

An up-and-coming New York *Times* reporter fabricates facts, and heads roll

ONE JOURNALIST CALLED IT A "low point in the 152-year history" of America's most celebrated newspaper, the New York *Times*. The journalist was a *Times* reporter, writing about his own paper in a front-page story that chronicled (in 7,165 words) the journalistic malfeasance of one of the publication's rising reporters, Jayson Blair, 27. According to the *Times's* investigation, Blair "fabricated comments. He concocted scenes. He lifted material from other newspapers and wire services." He described the houses of grieving parents he never visited, the nightmares of wounded soldiers who deny discussing them, the tears of people who seldom cry. "It's a huge black eye," said publisher Arthur Ochs Sulzberger Jr., whose family has controlled the paper since 1896.

The shock of Blair's lies ran deep: within a few weeks, the scandal opened fault lines in the newsroom of the paper and brought down the two men who had presided over the debacle, executive editor Howell Raines and his No. 2, managing editor Gerald Boyd. It was an unprecedented downfall at a major American newspaper—and again, the dual resignation couldn't be hushed up: it was reported on the front page of the *Times*.

Under Raines' hard-driving leadership, the *Times* had excelled in its coverage of news in the past two years. Raines took over the paper only six days before the biggest story in years, the terror attacks of 9/11, and his strategy of "flooding the zone" with reporters made the *Times* re-

OUT: The falsehoods of Blair, right, brought down top editor Raines, who announces he will resign, above. Behind him is publisher Sulzberger; No. 2 editor Boyd is at right

porting on the tragedy unparalleled. The paper won seven Pulitzer Prizes in 2002. But along the way, Raines infuriated reporters and editors, who complained that he favored a small coterie of star writers, pushed workers beyond reasonable limits and ruled by fear. He launched a crusade against the Augusta National Golf Club for its exclusion of women and then was partially responsible for the killing of columns by two respected sportswriters that didn't hew to his position on the matter.

Sulzberger stood by Raines at first, saying he would prefer not to accept his resignation. But Sulzberger also took an aggressive role in trying to gauge newsroom discontent, including holding a meeting of hundreds of employees in a Times Square theater—which made it clear that Raines and Boyd needed to act very fast to fix morale.

Then came a second scandal: Rick Bragg, a Pulitzer-prizewinning feature writer, was suspended after he filed a story about oystermen in Florida that had been largely reported by an uncredited intern. Bragg resigned, but further enraged the newsroom by claiming that the *Times's* national reporters did things like that all the time. When Raines issued a mild, tardy response, many of his writers felt he had sold them out. With outrage mounting against them, Raines and Boyd resigned; Sulzberger asked Joseph Lelyveld, a measured manager who is liked in the newsroom, to take over the paper on an interim basis.

Whether or not this was a scandal born of ambition and ego, it was also a story about race. Publications like the *Times* work hard to find and keep the best black reporters. Was Blair given special treatment because, like Boyd, he is black? Some colleagues charged he got second chances that others might not have. Others denied that race ensured his rise or delayed his fall. Variously described as charming and cunning, ambitious and lazy, Blair issued a statement claiming he had been "struggling with recurring personal issues." Those issues are now as public as you can get—you can read all about it in the newspaper of record.

> **❝ [Blair] fabricated comments. He concocted scenes. He lifted material. ❞**
>
> **—THE NEW YORK *TIMES***

Weak Links in the Chain of Command

Charges of rape and sexual harassment rock the Air Force Academy

BRING ME MEN," SAID THE TWO-FOOT-HIGH LETTERS inlaid into a stone arch at the U.S. Air Force Academy in Colorado Springs, Colo. Since 1964, every incoming class of cadets had marched beneath these words taken from an 1894 poem by Sam Walter Foss. But the sign came down in the spring of 2003. Foss's words were removed, along with the five top Air Force officers at the academy, in response to a burgeoning scandal involving dozens of incidents of rape and sexual assault against female cadets stretching back over the past decade.

The scandal broke when an investigative report, aired by Denver's local ABC affiliate, KMGH, revealed in February that five female cadets who had come forward to report

female cadets. Three months later, the new superintendent of the academy, General John Rosa, warned it could take years to change the school's culture, saying, "If you think you can come into an organization as complex as this is and do something in a month, you're fooling yourself."

In a sharp reversal of long-standing policy, the Air Force in October said it would grant anonymity to female cadets who alleged they had been assaulted. This was one of the reforms urged by the Fowler committee, which issued a scathing report the month before, noting that "the highest levels of leadership had information about serious problems at the academy, yet failed to take effective action." Perhaps the academy's arch should read, BRING US LEADERS. ■

❝ The highest levels of leadership ... failed to take effective action. ❞ — FOWLER COMMITTEE

having been sexually assaulted were subsequently disciplined or intimidated by superiors. Within weeks, seven more current and former cadets lodged similar complaints with Colorado's Representatives in Congress. Critics of the military charged that the armed forces had not responded to the Navy's Tailhook sex-abuse scandal of the early 1990s by creating a culture that scorned gender crimes and punished those who commit them.

In 1993 the Air Force Academy launched a program touted as a model for teaching character, and three years later it instituted a rape-crisis hot line run by cadets. The academy claims fewer than 100 calls were placed to the hot line between 1996 and 2002, but this may be because some cadets went to civilian rape-crisis centers. A center in Colorado Springs said it had counseled at least 22 cadets over the past 15 years, including one who was gang-raped. In the seven years before 2003, only 20 cases of sexual assault had been formally investigated at the school, leading to the dismissal of eight male cadets.

The Air Force's top general, John Jumper, soon acknowledged that the process for reporting abuse was failing and that "intimidation in the chain of command" may have kept women silent. But now the code of silence had been broken. Soon, the number of women alleging they had been raped at the Air Force Academy rose to 20, and a previously unreleased 1997 study by the Air Force revealed that 10% of all female cadets claimed they had been raped while at the academy and that 3 out of 4 of all female cadets said they would not report a rape for fear of reprisal. These estimates were later updated and revised slightly upward by the Defense Department's inspector general. A subsequent study, released at the end of March, indicated that 167 cadets claimed they had been sexually assaulted at the academy in 2001; there were 80 such claims in 2002.

In May an independent seven-member investigating committee under Florida Congresswoman Tillie Fowler uncovered 40 more allegations of sexual assault against

DAVID ZICKL FOR TIME

ACCUSER: Sharon Fullilove, a former cadet, claims she was raped by an upperclassman at the academy; she then left the school. "It's the good-ole-boy society," she charges

FADS, FOIBLES AND FANCIES

There's more to a year—happily—than bureaucrats, bombs and blackouts. To get a real feel for our moment in time, you have to know what we're wearing, how we're playing, what looks cool—and what's for dessert

INDOOR WATERPARKS
Summer's over, but it's always playtime inside the growing ranks of indoor waterparks. Some 45 are out there now; a dozen more are on the way

WORKING OUT

EXPEDITION RACES
These multidiscipline endurance contests, long popular with Aussies and Kiwis, are the new rage in America. Races involve teams of three or four people and can last hours—or days. Canoe, climb, clamber ... collapse!

SPAS FOR KIDS
Once the domain of adults, spas are wooing the under-18 set, hoping to grab some of the $20 billion spent on appearance each year by 33 million U.S. teens

POOL
The smoke ... the bets ... the brews ... the "boys" ... not. This isn't your grandpa's pool hall; a growing number of kid-friendly pool parlors offer video games, karaoke and jukeboxes. Rack 'em up!

KICKBALL
The old recess favorite is back, this time for adults. One league boasts more than 300 teams in 10 cities catering to more than 10,000 kickers. The sport unites baseball rules with soccer skills. Goal! ... er ... homer!

GOURMET HOT DOGS
Upscaling a ballpark classic, chefs are fixing up fancy franks. The 10-topping Chicago-style dog above is sold from a cart outside New York City's Eleven Madison Park restaurant

HOOKAHS
With all eyes on the Arab world, cool cats on campuses and at urban cafés are chewing the fat around a hookah, the ancient Middle Eastern water pipe filled with sweetened tobacco. Price: about $10 a pipeful

CHOWING DOWN

FLAVORED VODKAS
Neutral? That was your father's vodka. Today's hottest brands sport surprising new aromas and tastes, from hints of French grapes and vanilla to winter wheat, rye and citrus

FLAVORED MILK
Milk consumption is growing among people of all ages, and dairy companies are cooking up wild new flavors: amaretto, strawberry, coffee, peach and blueberry. Tip: stick to the low-fat versions

FONDUE
It's back! Thanks to the success of the Atkins diet, cheese is a hot health food, and once again it's hip to dip your bread into a pot of bubbling Gruyère

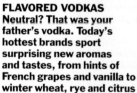

EXTREME ICE CREAM
Vanilla? How dreary! Exotic flavors are the new dream in cream. Choices include beer, lavender, rice, green grape and (get ready) Texas Goat Fromage Blanc & Roasted Hazelnuts

MANGOS
The fruit of the year? The mango, one of the most popular fruits around the planet, is finally catching on in the U.S. Use them in salads and salsas; peak season is May to September

SPORT JERSEYS
Dress like the pros—the NBA pros. Sport jerseys are coming out of the locker room and onto the runway, refitted and restyled for women as dresses. Leading the way: hip-hop star Eve, left, and singer Mariah Carey. Perspiration is optional

VINTAGE SNEAKERS
Retro collectible sneakers are a growing force in the athletic-shoe game, as exclusive, often unmarked rare-sneaks shops popped up nationwide. Dealers offer leftovers of old and discontinued models, a.k.a. deadstock. Never worn, never laced, rare Jordans like these can fetch as much as $1,000 on eBay

PAJAMAS
Dressing down? You can't get much more casual than not getting dressed at all—and many of us aren't bothering to get out of our sleepwear. Pajama bottoms are now worn everywhere, from the supermart to the shopping mall. From 2001 to '02, as apparel industry sales dropped 4%, pj sales jumped 34%

DRESSING UP

QLINK
This New Age version of the rabbit's foot is all the rage among highly superstitious professional golfers, and it's hitting the mainstream. The QLink is a lightweight pendant worn as a necklace that supposedly helps the body ward off bad electromagnetic fields and—well, whatever. Move over, i, X and e: Q is the new hot letter!

JELLY SHOES
The '80s are back—perhaps too soon—and so is the flexible plastic footwear of the *Footloose* era. Burberry offered a jelly thong sandal with its trademark plaid encased in transparent soles; the Melissa Love System jellied tennis shoe at left was the most popular style

SMALL PORTIONS
It's a graze craze: chefs are offering a wider variety of flavors served in smaller portions. Diners reduce calories—and costs. The mini-meal mantra: "Four bites and you're out"

QUIET PARTIES
Shhhh! The first Quiet Party took place in November 2002; now the idea is spreading. The rules: no talking above a whisper; cell phones are forbidden; the jukebox is muted. Need to chat? Write a note—or contribute to an ongoing chain story

DINING OUT

TABLE-SIDE COOKING
Retro restaurants are reviving a chestnut of old-time haute cuisine—they're slicing, saucing, dicing, deboning and flambéing right at the table. On the menu: Caesar salads, Dover sole and flaming steak. For dessert—what else? Flaming bananas Foster

GOING IN STYLE

Funeral and burial customs are getting a makeover as aging baby boomers begin preparing for death. For many, the emphasis is now on celebrating a life rather than mourning a death. Harleys and Corvettes lead processions in place of hearses; wakes are staged as garden parties; cremated remains are fashioned into jewelry, even stuffed into fireworks for those who want to go out with a bang. "We look at ourselves as being in the hospitality industry," a funeral director told TIME. With cremation surging in popularity, custom-designed containers for ashes are starting to appear. Ernie Wolfe, a Los Angeles art dealer, plans to have his ashes encased in the 10-ft. lobster-shaped casket at right. As last rites go, that's thinking outside the box

TABLOIDS ON STEROIDS

SAY "AAAHHHH"
The eye-opening, mouth-opening kiss of the year? Honors—if that's the right word—have to go to Spears and mentor Madonna, who smooched at the MTV Video Music Awards. Between them, they've gone through enough bustiers, garter belts and corsets to stock a Victoria's Secret outlet store. Something new was called for, and a hint of lesbianism—however fake—still makes for a great photo op. And to think Madonna was once able to shock us with her **BOY TOY** belt buckle

BRITNEY SPEARS & MADONNA

JULIE JACOBSON—AP/WIDE WORLD

PRINCE CHARLES

ALPHA—GLOBE PHOTOS

ROYAL PAIN
One headline screamed: "IS CHARLES BISEXUAL?" The answer, in small type: "Of course not." It was a tough year for Britain's Crown Prince, who faced a vague charge of sexual high jinks and new stories about his life with Princess Di, courtesy of her butler

■ Gossip! Scandal! Dirt! As America's infatuation with celebrity culture swells, the

PHIL SPECTOR

LORI SHEPLER—LA TIMES

TROUBLE IN NEVERLAND?
Sorry, no laughs here. In November, "King of Pop" Michael Jackson was charged with multiple counts of child molesting by law enforcement officials in Santa Barbara County, Cal. Authorities swooped down on the star's sprawling Neverland ranch on Nov. 19 and conducted a search of the property. Jackson declared his innocence and surrendered to officials on Nov. 20.

LISA MARIE PRESLEY

GASS ARROYO—AP/WIDE WORLD

BOTTOM OF THE POPS
The first superstar record producer, Spector, 63, has lived in seclusion for years, as stories of his eccentricities spread. In February, B-movie actress Lana Clarkson was found dead in his Los Angeles mansion, shot in the head and neck. Taken into custody, Spector was released on $1 million bail

MICHAEL JACKSON

CARLO ALLEGRI—GETTY IMAGES

THE DAUGHTER ALSO RISES
If you've survived marriages to Michael Jackson and Nicolas Cage, you're probably equipped to face the world's music critics. Lisa Marie Presley, 35, picked up where Dad left off on her debut CD, *To Whom It May Concern*

SPLITTING UP

JENNIFER GRAYLOCK—AP/WIDE WORLD

JENNIFER LOPEZ & BEN AFFLECK

WEDDING BELL BLUES
The stars the tabloids call "Bennifer" were four days from the altar in September when they abruptly called off the gaudy affair, saying, "When we found ourselves … contemplating hiring three separate 'decoy brides' at three different locations, we realized that something was awry." Too bad Ben, 31, and J-Lo, 33, didn't pull the plug on their flop movie, *Gigli*

CHRIS PIZZELLO—AP/WIDE WORLD

KID ROCK & PAMELA ANDERSON

DEPT. OF DOMESTIC ABUSE
The favors at their lavish March 2002 wedding were satin candy boxes reading, LIZA AND DAVID 4 EVER. Those satin candy boxes lied! Producer Gest, 50, filed for divorce from Liza-with-a-Z, 57, in August, claiming she had beaten him—the brute!

YUI MOK—PA/EPA/WIDE WORLD

DAVID GEST & LIZA MINNELLI

LOW-RENT ROMANTICS
Rock, 32, the T shirt–wearing, greasy-locked avatar of trailer-park chic and Anderson, 36, the bosom-enhanced former star of *Baywatch* (and a notorious porn home video), kept the tabloids busy in 2003. Splitting up, making up, splitting again—whew! At year's end Pamela seemed to be spending her quality time with ex-hubby Tommy Lee

gossip mills need fodder. Here are the top stars of the checkout lanes in 2003 ▪

AMY GRAVES—FWD/WIDE WORLD

HARRISON FORD & CALISTA FLOCKHART

OLDER MAN, YOUNGER WOMAN
Well, here's the skinny on TV's Ally McBeal, 39, and film's Indiana Jones, 61: they're a pair. Ford, a grandfather of two and father of four, is playing papa to McBeal's son Liam, now 3

KUTCHY-KOO!
Since her 1998 separation from actor Bruce Willis, Moore has eschewed the spotlight, living quietly with her three girls in Idaho. But when the star, now 41, decided to revive her movie career, she needed an accessory—and revved up the publicity by snagging Kutcher, the 25-year-old star of TV's *That 70s Show*

HOOKING UP

TAMMI ARROYO—AP/WIDE WORLD

DEMI MOORE & ASHTON KUTCHER

JENNIFER GRAYLOCK—AP/WIDE WORLD

DIANE KRALL & ELVIS COSTELLO

OLDIES MAN, OLDIES WOMAN
These two aren't the usual tabloid fodder, but when the geekiest guy of the '80s New Wave craze, now 48, began squiring around the jazz world's sultriest vocalist, 39—well, pump it up! The musicians said they would marry; meanwhile, Elvis sang love ballads on a new CD, *North*

N O T E B O O K

Images

Digital Dada

The fad of the year? The flash mob. One of the first social constructs of the cell-phone age, it's a quick summons to assemble in a random location and engage in a pointless activity, like the folks in London at right. The rage began in New York City and soon went global. Why? Because we can!

SCOTT BARBOUR—GETTY IMAGES

ONLINE: Students hit the computers at wireless Collegiate

TED THAI FOR TIME

The Unwired Classroom

The latest trend in computerized schools? Wireless technology. At the private Packer Collegiate Institute in Brooklyn, N.Y., students from Level 6 on are issued laptops, and some 50 wireless stations on the campus keep kids online constantly. Homework and classwork are performed online, though tests are taken on paper, since students can grab answers off the Internet. There's a virtual lost-and-found bulletin board and another one for opinions on Iraq. Last year the school set up an electronic link with a laptop school on an Indian reservation in Alaska, and the kids swapped poems and pictures of themselves.

Verdict: Affirmative

In a surprising turn of events in America's ongoing battle over affirmative action, the Supreme Court in June upheld the right of universities to consider race in admissions procedures in order to achieve a diverse student body. In two lawsuits challenging admission policies at the University of Michigan, the court ruled 5 to 4 in favor of the University's Law School policy and, by a vote of 6 to 3, reversed, in part, its undergraduate policy, while still allowing for attention to race in admissions. Justice Sandra Day O'Connor, a centrist and swing vote on the court, wrote the majority opinion in the Law School case; generally conservative Chief Justice William Rehnquist wrote the majority opinion in the undergraduate case. The court had been widely expected to rule against the university.

ADMIT IT BUSH YOU FEAR BLACK SUCCESS!

RICK BOWMER—AP/WIDE WORLD

YES! Protesters rally in Washington

■ PROFILE

JACQUES BRINON—AP/WIDE WORLD

LOUISEAU: A tragedy in France

Shadow of a Falling Star

French chef Bernard Louiseau, 52, ran one of only 25 restaurants in France awarded three stars by the all-powerful Michelin guide. His Côte d'Or restaurant in Burgundy was a gourmand's shrine. Louiseau had become perhaps France's most famous chef, a TV star who sold a line of soups, champagne, even perfume. But when the respected GaultMillau guide inexplicably reduced his ranking early in 2003, the great chef put a gun in his mouth and committed suicide.

Anniversaries

Aviation 100 Years

Mt. Everest 50 Years

DNA 50 Years

To Defy Gravity's

Celebrating the centennial of the first powered flight, we salute aviation's pioneers: magnificent men—and women—and their flying machines

THE SAND DUNES AT KITTY HAWK ON NORTH CAROLINA'S Outer Banks were windy and chilly on Dec. 17, 1903, the day a pair of bicycle-shop owners from Ohio became the first humans to achieve powered flight. It would be nice to record that sizable crowds gathered and roared with acclaim as Orville and Wilbur Wright's flying machine soared—briefly—aloft. But there was no crowd, and at least one spectator went away disappointed: a local undertaker had watched the proceedings from a horse-drawn buggy, on the chance that a business opportunity might present itself.

The first flight, with Orville at the controls, lasted just 12 seconds, and the airplane traveled only 120 ft. across the sand. But before the day was over, the brothers' *Flyer 1* managed a flight of 59 seconds and 852 ft., with Wilbur as pilot. The Wrights and mankind never looked back. The next 50 years were aviation's heroic age, as a fascinating cast of characters—test pilots, adventurers, engineers and executives—drove the science and commerce of flight forward. Recalling the achievements of these aviation pioneers seems an appropriate way to celebrate the centennial of flight.

The Wrights are sometimes portrayed as little more than inspired tinkerers; this simplification suits a favorite American narrative, the triumph of the humble amateur over the calculating professional. In fact, the brothers' dreams of flight were rooted in the scientific method. *Flyer 1's* design was tested in a wind tunnel designed by the brothers in order to study aerodynamics; it was one of the first such devices. In their experiments, working with models, the brothers discovered the key principles that allowed them to be first in the worldwide race to achieve powered flight: a long, narrow wing, tapering from front to back, is the best shape to provide lift; the propeller could serve as a sort of rotating wing to generate further lift; a forward horizontal rudder could control the up-and-down pitch of the craft in flight, while twin vertical rudders in the rear could manage its side-to-side yaw. When conventional petroleum-powered engines proved too heavy for their craft, they designed an innovative 12-h.p. engine that weighed only 152 lbs.

The result was a sort of skeleton airplane made of spruce, ash and muslin, with a 40-ft. wingspan—a flying example of form following function. On Dec. 18, only four

BETTMANN/CORBIS

Samuel Langley
The head of the Smithsonian Institution was a friendly rival of the Wrights'. But when his Great Aerodrome, above, failed to carry a pilot aloft, he was ridiculed and his craft dubbed "Langley's Folly"

The Wright Brothers
Orville was at the controls when the 600-lb. *Flyer 1* first took to the skies, for all of 12 seconds. They accomplished three other successful flights on Dec. 17, 1903. Only three days before, the brothers had failed to get the craft off the ground

Grasp

Igor Sikorsky

The Russian-born engineer pioneered a different take on flight; the rotor-powered helicopter. Above, he's at the controls as his VS-300 helicopter breaks a world record in 1941, hovering for 1 hr. 32 min.

Amelia Earhart

In 1928 "Lady Lindy" was a passenger on a three-person plane that crossed the Atlantic; four years later she became the first person since Lindbergh to make that trip solo. In 1937 Earhart's plane was lost in the Pacific Ocean as she attempted a round-the-world trip

Glenn Curtiss & HenryFord

Curtiss, a former bike-shop owner, was the leading aircraft-maker in the U.S. by 1914. "The Father of Naval Aviation" built the first flying boats. Auto magnate Henry Ford, a fellow flying buff, joined him in 1915, right

Santos DuMont

The wealthy Brazilian, above, is one of the most fascinating figures of early aviation. Living in Paris, he began his research by flying dirigibles, then began to design planes like this 1907 model

Charles Lindbergh

The son of a Minnesota Congressman was only 25 when his solo flight to Paris made him the most celebrated man of his age—a role the introverted pilot came to hate

U.S. newspapers carried accounts of the previous day's historic event; the reports were widely disbelieved. But as rivals and imitators mastered the Wrights' new principles of flight, aircraft began taking to the skies around the world. Aviation, born so soon after the turn of the 20th century, became a mighty motor in shaping it. In shattering old constraints of distance, powered flight also altered mankind's sense of time even as it was revolutionizing warfare, commerce and society.

World War I hot-wired the aviation world, accelerating the evolution of technology and compressing into a single five-year span design innovations that might have taken decades. Yet even after the war, flying remained the arena of barnstormers and experimenters, a novelty rather than a necessity. Aviation pioneers like Glenn Curtiss continued to develop planes that flew faster and farther, even ones that landed on water. But it wasn't until a former barnstormer, Charles Lindbergh, ignited the world's imagination with his solo flight across the Atlantic in 1927 that visionaries began to glimpse aviation's potential as a means of conveyance, a rival to the railroad and automobile in moving freight and people.

The 1930s, although buffeted by economic depression, saw enormous growth in aviation. A host of airline companies spread their wings (though many soon folded them, in a mayfly's brief life-span). Air-mail delivery accelerated communication and commerce. And when the brilliant designer Donald Douglas unveiled his milestone DC-3—with its quiet, pressurized cabin, tricycle landing gear and advanced navigation systems—aviation emerged from its early days, and airline travel became feasible for a much broader group of individuals.

Like the first global war 25 years before it, World War II spurred major advances in flight. The father of the automotive assembly line, Henry Ford, was pressed into duty; his giant Michigan factories began turning out massive bombers by the hundreds. Aircraft designers began working with new jet propulsion systems that generated forward thrust by forcing heated air through turbines. A few prototypes were being tested by war's end. But it wasn't until the Korean War in the early 1950s that jet fighters began to dominate the skies. Meanwhile, a courageous U.S. military test pilot, Chuck Yeager, became the first human to fly faster than the speed of sound; his flight in a rocket-powered experimental craft effectively opened the space age.

The 1950s saw the introduction of the first passenger jets. American manufacturer William Boeing's company led the way with the Boeing 707, which carried its first customers in 1958. Twelve years later, the 707 was dwarfed by Boeing's gigantic people hauler, the 747. It is a measure of the rapidity of the evolution of aviation technology that the greatest hero of flying's early days, Lindbergh, served as an adviser to Boeing on the design of the 747. Another measure: the 747's 195-ft. wingspan was 75 ft. longer than the length of *Flyer 1*'s first flight.

Museums, airlines, aviation societies, governments, Sunday pilots and hangar hounds of all stripes paused in 2003 to celebrate the 100th anniversary of aviation and to salute the Wright brothers. The Smithsonian's Air and Space Museum hauled *Flyer 1* down from the rafters and displayed it in a place of honor. Pilots trained to fly exact models of the craft; the U.S. Postal Service issued a stamp; and on Dec. 17, Kitty Hawk filled up with cheering throngs for the official observance of that day 100 years before, when the dunes were empty but the sky was not, and the undertaker went home disappointed. ■

Douglas DC-3
Move over, Flyer 1. When Donald Douglas' DC-3 began flying in 1936, aviation entered a new phase. Comfortable and quiet, the streamlined craft made flying feasible for everyone and ushered in the airline age

Donald Douglas
Hooked on flight after seeing an Orville Wright demonstration for the Army in 1908, Douglas left the U.S. Naval Academy to study aeronautical engineering. His landmark DC-3 was the dominant plane in the skies for more than 20 years, beginning in 1936, until it was eclipsed by Boeing's 707 jet in 1958

HULTON ARCHIVE—GETTY IMAGES

Howard Hughes
The wealthy manufacturing heir never thought small: he parlayed his fortune into a career as a Hollywood mogul. His mammoth flying boat, the eight-engine Spruce Goose, a collaboration with industrialist Henry Kaiser, was designed as a cargo and troop hauler. It flew only once, in November 1947

William Boeing
One of those who transformed aviation from a novelty into an industry, the son of a wealthy timber merchant became entranced with flight after seeing an early airplane in 1909. His company built planes for the government in World War I, then led in the growth of air mail and the airline industry in the 1920s and '30s. In love with speed, he retired from aviation to breed racehorses

PH-ALI

TSCHAPPY

Chuck Yeager
Writer Tom Wolfe traced the detached yet omniscient voice issuing from a thousand flight decks to the West Virginia test pilot, whose "aw-shucks" humility became aviation's ideal of grace under pressure. Yeager soared through the so-called sound barrier in 1947

EAA—GETTY IMAGES

BETTMANN/CORBIS

Ready for Their 12 Seconds of Fame
Gearing up to re-create history, pilots gather in front of a replica of the Wrights' Flyer 1 at the famed annual aviation show in Oshkosh, Wis., in July 2003. The plane was built by the Experimental Aircraft Association, a participant in the year-long celebration of aviation's centennial. At left is famed test pilot Scott Crossfield, with trainees Ken Hyde, Kevin Kochersberger, Terry Queijo and Chris Johnson

An unlikely pair of trailblazers mapped the elegant messenger of heredity

O NE OF THE MOST INFLUENTIAL DISCOVERIES IN THE history of biology was announced in a sentence now famed for its understatement. In a one-page letter that ran in the science journal *Nature* on April 25, 1953, Briton Francis Crick and American James Watson stated, "We wish to suggest a structure for the salt of deoxyribose nucleic acid (D.N.A.). This structure has novel features which are of considerable biological interest."

Considerable interest, indeed. In fact, the deciphering of this single molecule, which carries the recipe for how to put together a human being from scratch, launched a revolution that—after 50 years—is still in its infancy. The work of Watson and Crick has influenced the drugs we take, the food we eat, the way we establish guilt or innocence, even the choices we face when we decide to have a baby.

Call it a twist of fate: the elegant pairing of DNA's double helix structure was first defined by an inelegant pair of researchers who beat a number of brilliant scientists to the prize. Francis Crick, 36 in 1953, was an egotistical, acerbic physicist. James Watson, then 25, was brash, confident and fame hungry. They weren't the most experienced scientists in the contest; they didn't have the best equipment and didn't even know much biochemistry. Yet with a crucial assist from Briton Rosalind Franklin—a rival whose pioneering work with a form of imaging called X-ray crystallography gave them significant clues—the two managed to create the first model of the DNA molecule. They showed how DNA's form mirrored its function; the double helix is a self-reproducing molecule that "unzips" along its length, unraveling into two half-ladders that are reverse images of each other. Then each half rebuilds itself from components stored in the cell.

With their breakthrough, the two young men scooped their chief rival, the American chemist Linus Pauling, who was also hot on the trail of DNA. The entire story is well told in Watson's memoir, *The Double Helix* (1968), which captures the complex emotions—curiosity, vanity, envy—that drive scientists at the highest level. Following their success, Crick went on to do significant research on proteins and human consciousness. Watson turned to administration, leading the important work on gene research performed at the Cold Spring Harbor Laboratory on Long Island, N.Y., then helping establish the groundbreaking Human Genome Project. As he told TIME, in recalling the 50th anniversary of the breakthrough, "We have more frontiers now than when I was getting started." If so, it's thanks to this most unlikely pair of pathfinders, the Lewis and Clark of biochemistry. ∎

The Double Helix
James Watson, left, and Francis Crick in 1953, with their original model of the double helix. Above, Watson, on right, discusses DNA at a 2003 TIME conference that observed the 50th anniversary of his and Crick's discovery

To Chart the Shape of Life

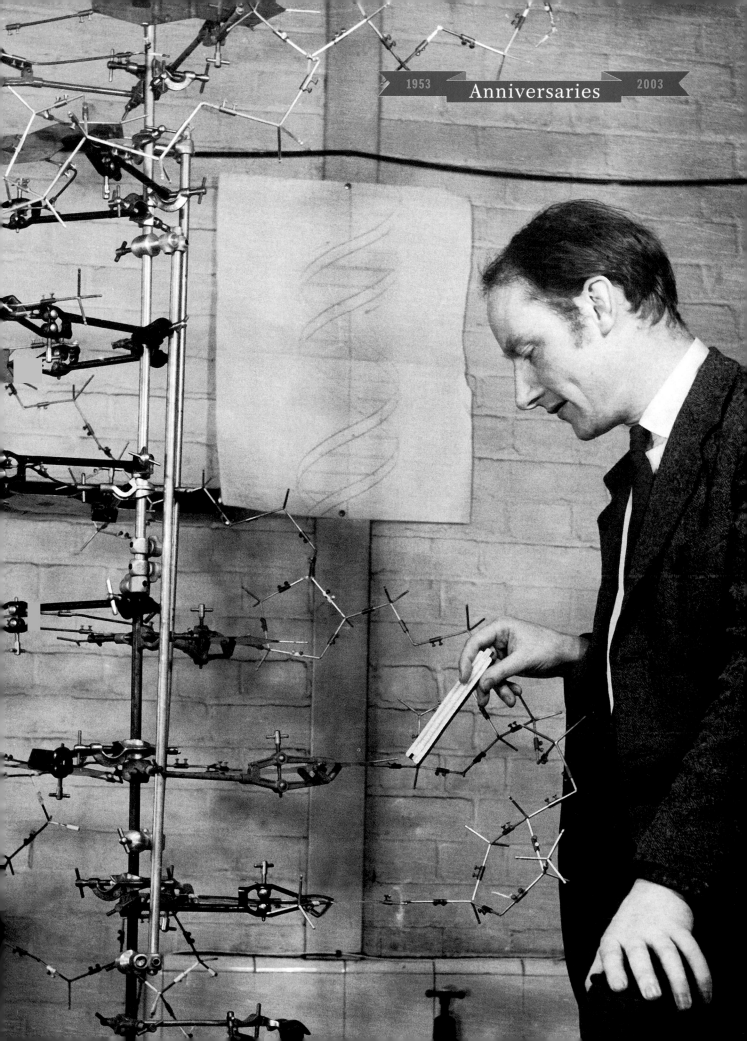

To Stand Atop the

A tough Kiwi and a stalwart Sherpa were first to climb the world's highest mountain. This story is condensed from TIME's original 1953 account

A MAN HAS NOT LONG TO LIVE ABOVE 22,000 FT. HIS heart dilates and beats faster; he has no desire to eat. The thin air leaves him gasping; the cold that numbs his limbs fills his throat with lumps of mucus, can sap his courage so that every step forward demands a conscious effort of will to jog the body on.

Camp V was at 22,500 ft. at the head of the Western Cwm. Here the South Col rose 3,000 ft. sheer. Ice boots were changed for footwear soled with microcellular rubber (to keep out –50° cold). Goggles protected the men from snow blindness; padded smocks enclosed their bodies. One by one, Hunt and Hillary, Bourdillon and Evans, Noyce, Wilson and Tenzing, put on their oxygen masks and learned to sleep in them.

Thus, fully accoutered, they struck at the face of Lhotse [Everest's neighbor]. Heavy icing is dangerous on a slope of 30°; Lhotse in many places is close to vertical. Wilfred Noyce, a schoolmaster, took two days to hack an ice stair-

case diagonally up to the col. Camp VI and Camp VII were established on the face; finally, Noyce and a Sherpa gang reached the col and stood in a clear sky on the threshold of Everest. Here they made Camp VIII at 25,850 ft. The last climb was 3,000 ft. No one man could have tried it if [expedition leader John] Hunt had not planned well. In the last exhausting stages, two assault teams (two men to each) had been "babied" for the final attack. Team No. 1 got the order to go.

Tom Bourdillon, a nuclear physicist, and Charles Evans, a Liverpool physician, went up from Camp

World

A Distant Goal

The 1953 British expedition, led by John Hunt, was the eighth to attempt to climb Everest (the peak at right) since 1921, when Tibet first granted access to the mountain to outsiders. Among those who failed to reach the summit was George ("Because It's There") Mallory, who died on the mountain in 1924. His body was finally located on Everest in 1999

VIII toward the halfway mark—a rounded shoulder of rock known as the South Summit. Stumbling and panting, they made it and vanished in the cloud beyond. No man had been higher and lived, but the pair lacked strength to go on. Back they came.

Team No. 2 was [Edmund] Hillary, the beekeeper from Auckland, New Zealand, and Tenzing [Norgay], the sinewy Asian whom Colonel Hunt named "the greatest Sherpa of them all." They dragged themselves up to 27,900 ft. and there, on a rocky ledge, they spent a gale-swept night in a ragged tent.

Dawn on May 20 made the Himalayas glow. At 6:30 they thawed out their boots and buckled on all that remained of the precious oxygen. The summit was hidden in cloud, but they knew it lay ahead and above. On and up they stumbled, like flies on a whitewashed wall. An unmapped ice ridge stopped them, as it had stopped Team No. 1. On one side, the ridge's gables projected over a face that fell 12,000 ft. Opposite was snow, firm enough for footholds but guarded by a sheer rock face 40 ft. high and holdless. At sea level this would be a minor obstacle to a trained mountaineer, but at 29,000 ft., neither Hillary nor Tenzing could attempt it. Instead they found a chimney that opened to the top. Hillary went first and scrabbled his way upward through the chimney, using shoulders and knees as levers. Then it was Tenzing's turn, and soon the pair lay together in the frozen snow at the top. They got up and plodded on. As fast as one hump was cleared, the next blocked the view. Both men were slowing down when

A Long Way Down
Back from the summit, trailblazers Tenzing, left, and Hillary catch their breath and take nourishment

suddenly it loomed into view—one last narrow snow ridge running up to a peak beyond which nothing was higher.

They made it, roped together, and stood on the roof of the world. It was exactly 11:30 a.m. on Friday, May 20, 1953. Gravely they shook hands, and Tenzing, forgetting formality, hugged Hillary like a bear. Then they took photographs of the British, Nepalese, Indian and U.N. flags lashed to Tenzing's icepick. What did it feel like to be there? Said Hillary: "Damn good." Tenzing, a devout Buddhist, said, "I thought of God and the greatness of His work." ∎

A Jolly Good Fellow
Hillary, 83 in 2003, basks in the adulation of the crowd during a parade in Kathmandu, Nepal, marking the 50th anniversary of the climb. Tenzing Norgay died in 1986

Alone at the Top
Hillary took this picture of Norgay, his ice pick fluttering with flags, in their first moments atop Everest. Forty-three years later, Norgay's son Jamling would follow his father's footsteps to stand at the mountain's peak

No Joy in Wrigleyville

The most memorable play of 2003—in any sport—didn't involve an athlete. Instead, it was made by Chicago Cubs fan Steve Bartman, 26, the chap in the blue hat, who reached for a foul fly ball hit by the Florida Marlins' Luis Castillo, spoiling Cubs outfielder Moises Alou's chance to catch the fly and put the brakes on a Marlins rally. No go. The Cubs, one of the two major league teams with a history of breaking the hearts of their fans, at this point were only five outs away from winning their league championship series against the Marlins and going to the World Series for the first time since 1945. But they managed to lose. And as for the other team of heartbreakers, the doomed Boston Red Sox—well, would you believe they also got within five outs of winning their championship series against the hated New York Yankees and then managed to lose too? You could look it up.

Sport

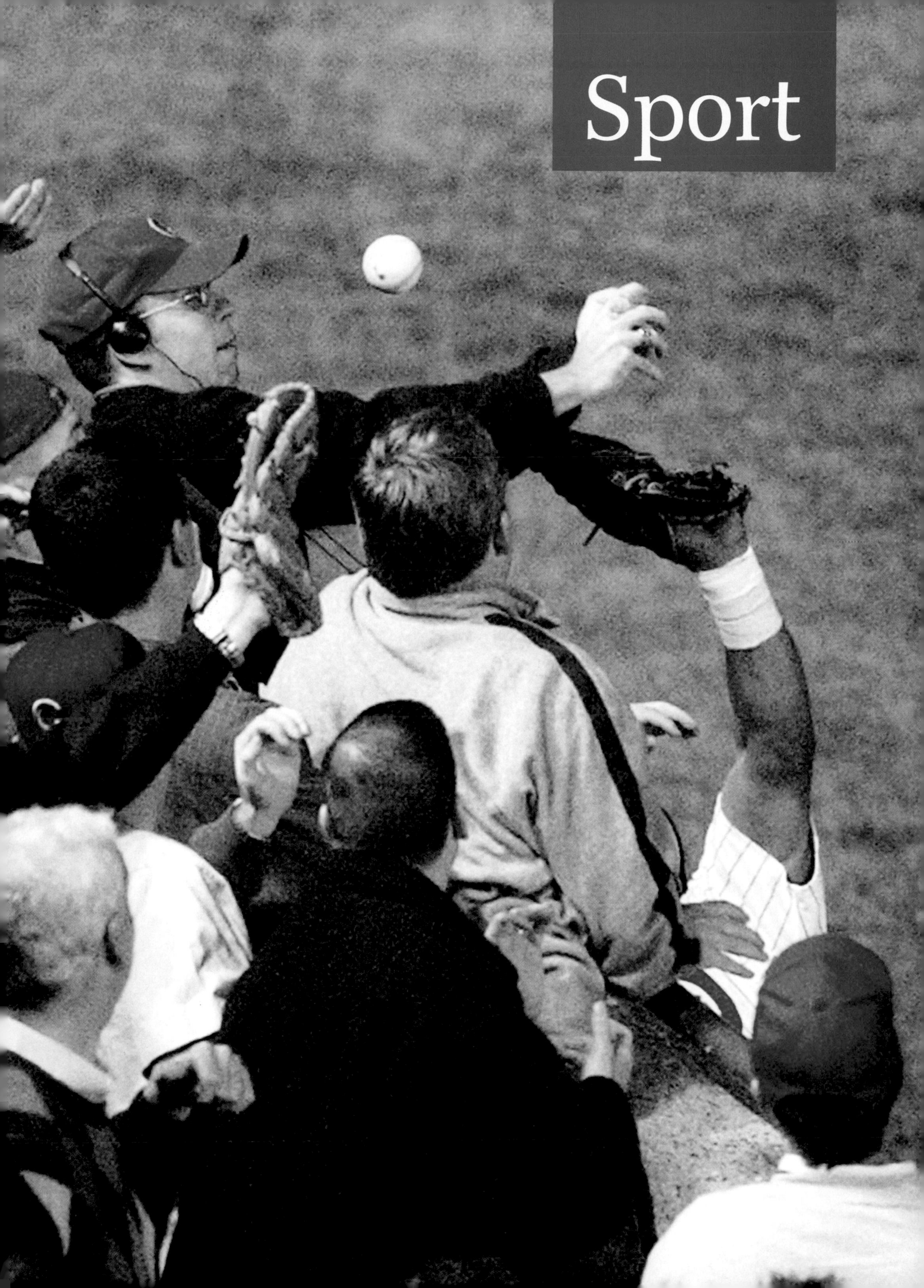

MASTERS CHAMPION
MIKE WEIR

BRITISH OPEN CHAMPION
BEN CURTIS

OUT OF THE WOODS

For the first year since he became a pro, Tiger Woods didn't win a major trophy, but his absence brought four fine players to the fore

SHERLOCK HOLMES ONCE NOTED THAT the most telling point at an alleged crime scene was the dog that didn't bark. For lovers of golf, the most memorable event of the 2003 season was the Tiger that didn't win a single major trophy. For the first time since 1998, a year after he won his first major event in unforgettable fashion, leading the Masters field by 12 strokes, Tiger Woods, 27, failed to win one of golf's four great challenges.

But, please, spare your tears for Tiger. Still ranked No. 1 in the world by a wide margin, Woods enjoyed a year that would have made any other golfer delirious with joy: he won five PGA tournaments, took home the PGA Player of the Year Award for the 5th straight year and was the tour's No. 2 money winner, earning $6.6 million.

The good news: the leader board abhors a vacuum, and when Woods didn't win a major trophy, four other fine golfers

CLOSE, NO CIGAR: Tiger's best performance in a major '03 event came at the British Open in July, where he tied for fourth place

got a chance to shine. Two of them were familiar to most fans; two were delightful surprises. And though TV executives may have regretted Woods' showing (ratings decline markedly when he doesn't contend), the four tournaments proved unforgettable, from the young unknown who won the venerable British Open to the journeyman who snagged the PGA trophy with a great chip shot on the last hole.

THE MASTERS. Mike Weir, 32, has been promising to break out as one of the game's top players for the past few years. The Canadian left-hander did just that in the Masters, going bogey-free on the final day to tie American Len Mattiace after 72 holes, then beating him on the first hole of a sudden-death playoff. Woods was gracious in giving Weir the winner's famous green jacket, especially since Weir had denied Woods the chance to become the first golfer ever to wear it three years in a row.

U.S. OPEN CHAMPION
JIM FURYK

P.G.A. CHAMPION
SHAUN MICHEEL

BRITISH OPEN. The old Royal St. George's course had never seen anything like this: American Ben Curtis, 26, an absolute unknown, became the first pro to win the tournament's claret jug on his first appearance in it since Tom Watson in 1975. Curtis, ranked No. 396 in the world, took home the title despite carding four bogeys in the last seven holes; his closest competitor, Thomas Bjorn of Denmark, had an even worse final nine, with a double bogey on the 16th hole effectively sealing his doom.

U.S. OPEN. Like Weir, Jim Furyk, 33, has long been regarded as one of the game's most promising players. He had finished in the Top 10 at 12 different major tournaments yet never higher than fourth. At the U.S. Open at the Olympia Fields course near Chicago, Furyk simply ran away from the field, finishing eight strokes under par and three strokes ahead of second-place Stephen Leaney—despite three-putting the final hole.

PGA CHAMPIONSHIP. Less than a month after Curtis won the British Open, another unfamiliar face, Shaun Micheel, 34, took the PGA championship at the Oak Hill course in Rochester, N.Y. Locked in a tough struggle with playing partner Chad Campbell, Micheel won the tournament on the final hole with a masterly shot, firing a 7-iron from 175 yards out to within two inches of the cup for a tap-in birdie and his first PGA win. It was a dramatic—and fitting—conclusion to the year of the up-and-comer in golf's most prestigious championships. We would summarize the result of the majors as Four Trophies and a Funeral, but no one thinks Tiger Woods is dead, though a few more of us are beginning to suspect he may be human. ■

PAUL BUCK—EPA/WIDE WORLD

■ TEEING UP VS. THE TEED OFF: ANNIKA SORENSTAM
There was no question who was golfer of the year in the women's game: Annika Sorenstam, 33, grabbed more attention than any other female pro in years when she announced she'd play in the PGA's Colonial Invitational tournament in Forth Worth, Texas, in May. The Swedish-born champion has dominated the LPGA tour in recent years, winning 19 tournaments in the past two alone. Most fans looked forward to seeing the LPGA's top player take on the world's best men, although a few spoilsports were annoyed, including top male pro Vijay Singh, who griped, "She doesn't belong out here." Sadly for those who were pulling for her, the usually steady Sorenstam didn't command her best game amid the media circus at the Colonial: she carded a 145 for 36 holes, missing the cut by four strokes.

LEADERS OF THE PACK

Break out the yellow jerseys and rewrite the record books: athletes old, young and in between made 2003 a memorable year on the racetrack, the hardwood and the diamond

ROGER CLEMENS
The hard-throwing right-hander, 41, said he'd retire after a magnificent 20-year career for Boston, Toronto and New York, though many fans hoped he'd change his mind. In 2003 he reached two milestones in one night: win No. 300 and strike-out No. 4,000 both came on June 13

SWIN CASH
In its brief—and still, sadly, a bit shaky—seven-year life, the Women's National Basketball Association has seen only two championship teams, the Houston Comets and L.A. Sparks. Not this year: in 2003 former U. Conn. star Cash, 24, led the Detroit Shock to the title over the Sparks

LANCE ARMSTRONG
Old news? Maybe so. But it wouldn't be fair to a magnificent athlete not to run a picture of his now familiar victory ride in cycling's greatest contest, the Tour de France. For the fifth year in a row, tying the record, the gritty cancer survivor wore the event's yellow jersey on its final day. But this time around, victory came harder. Armstrong, 31, didn't dominate, as he had in the past; he eked out victory by a margin of only 61 seconds. Lance's next goal: winning the 2004 race to become the only person to win the event six times in a row

FUNNY CIDE

When will horse racing have its first Triple Crown winner since 1978? In four of the past six years, horses had won the first two events, the Kentucky Derby and Preakness, only to fail in the Belmont Stakes. This year the surprising gelding Funny Cide did the same, winning the first two races but running third at Belmont. Maybe next year

GAIL BURTON—AP/WIDE WORLD

MICHAEL SCHUMACHER

NASCAR may rule U.S. auto racing, but Formula One is tops worldwide, and the German who drives for Ferrari is top dog. Below, he wins the Japan Grand Prix to become the first six-time World Champion

PAUL BUCK—EPA/WIDE WORLD

TIM DUNCAN AND DAVID ROBINSON

The "twin towers" and their San Antonio Spurs dominated Jason Kidd and the New Jersey Nets in six games to win the NBA title. Duncan, 27, notched 21 points, 20 rebounds, 10 assists and eight blocks in the last game, missing the fifth quadruple-double in NBA history by two blocks

SHIZUO KAMBAYASHI—AP/WIDE WORLD (2)

■ PROFILE

This Time It's for Real

MJ is retiring. Well, that's what he says. But anyone who has ever watched Michael Jordan's love affair with the game of basketball— and that's just about everybody— wonders if he means it this time around. After all, Jordan has retired not once but twice before. The first time, in 1994, he left the game at his absolute peak, after carrying the Chicago Bulls to three NBA titles in three straight years. When he returned to the game in 1996, after a rough two years in which he tried to become a professional baseball player, Jordan again took the Bulls to a three-peat. He retired again after the '98 season, but he isn't cut out to be a spectator. After becoming President of the lowly Washington Wizards, he soon was

JORDAN: Sweet career, sour aftertaste

back in uniform. During the next two years, he showed much of his old grace and court savvy—even as he served in the Wizards' front office— though it was clear his best playing days were behind him.

Sadly, Jordan's departure from the Wizards was an unhappy one: he got his walking papers in May after a rage-filled, 18-min. meeting with owner Abe Polin. But stay tuned, fans—the NFL can always find room for a good placekicker.

THIS WAY: Alex Gonzalez wins Game 4 of the Series with a 12th-inning home run

David 4, Goliath 2

Both the New York Yankees and Florida Marlins came into the 2003 World Series reeling a bit after the the incredible events of the league championship series, in which the Chicago Cubs and Boston Red Sox found inventive new ways to torment their fans. But both the Yanks and Marlins profited from having veteran managers. For New York's solid Joe Torre, it was the sixth Series in eight years. And though it was the first World Series for Florida's Jack McKeon, who took over the Marlins after the season began, his 50 years in the game showed in his calm, canny approach. At 72, he was the oldest manager ever to take part in a Series.

Torre's team was long—perhaps too long—on old hands like Bernie Williams, Andy Pettite and Derek Jeter. McKeon's Marlins had the edge in youth, vigor and attitude— and in Josh Beckett, 23, they had the hottest pitcher in baseball. The Marlins took the Series in six games, winning the last one at Yankee Stadium as Beckett pitched a three-hitter on three days' rest.

U.S. Yields Soccer Crown

Was it only four years ago that the U.S. women's soccer team beat China in the finals with Bill Clinton cheering them on, Brandi Chastain doffed her jersey, and America embraced its champions? Four years later, the Women's World Cup

UPSET: Mia Hamm and Chastain

returned to the U.S., hastily moved from China because of the SARS epidemic. The U.S. team started the tournament well, but in the semifinal it couldn't get its offense going against Germany; the U.S. lost 3-0. Next stop: the 2004 Summer Olympic Games.

Images

Say It Ain't So!

Los Angeles Lakers guard Kobe Bryant, 25, has always been one of the NBA's good guys. So fans were shocked when Bryant was indicted in July on charges that he had raped a 19-year-old college student working at a resort in Vail, Colo. At his first court date, on Aug. 6, defense attorney Pamela Mackey patted the star on the back, left. Bryant denied the charges but said he had committed adultery in the past.

Younger, Faster, Richer

Many great musicians began as child prodigies, and the stage has its tyro troupers. Now it seems that more and more sports are being rocked by youthquakes.

Soccer's brightest hope is gifted young Freddy Adu, who turned 14 early in 2003. In November the Ghanaian-born Adu signed to play with Major League Soccer in the U.S.; he may be the youngest athetle to play in a professional team sport in America since 14-year-old Fred Chapman played a form of professional baseball in 1887. Nike paid the phenom $1 million to endorse its soccer shoes.

Then there's LeBron James. At 18, the 6-ft. 8-in. James hit the jackpot. The NBA's No. 1 draft pick signed with the Cleveland Cavaliers right out of high school, for $13 million. Then (surprise!) Nike stepped in, offering him a seven-year endorsement deal worth more than $90 million. It may pay off: James scored in double figures for five of his first seven games.

Golfer Michelle Wie is still in her salad days; she graduated the 8th grade in 2003. To celebrate, she won the U.S. Women's Public Links Championship, which made her the youngest player ever to win a USGA event. Then she made the cut at the U.S. Women's Open. Though Michele can drive the ball 300 yds. off the tee, she still hasn't turned pro. Her new dream: to play in the Masters tournament in 2004.

ANTTI AIMO-KOIVISTO—LEHTIKUVA—AP/WIDE WORLD

ADU: Touted as the next Pelé—at 14

DUANE BURLESON—AP/WIDE WORLD

JAMES: From high school to the pros

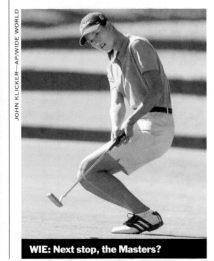

JOHN KLICKER—AP/WIDE WORLD

WIE: Next stop, the Masters?

Close Encounter

An observer trains a telescope on Mars from a perch atop the Miami Museum of Science on Aug. 27, as our nearest planetary neighbor made its closest pass to Earth in some 60,000 years. The Red Planet's flyby coincided with a boom in amateur sky watching in America: membership in astronomy clubs is soaring, and affordable new technology is allowing backyard stargazers to achieve glorious views—and professional-quality pictures—of the skies.

**Photograph by
Joe Raedle—Getty Images**

Science

THE LAST SONG THE LOST CREW OF THE SPACE SHUTTLE *Columbia* ever heard was *Scotland the Brave* by the 51st Highland Brigade. That was the wake-up song beamed up by NASA on Feb. 1, the morning the ship was supposed to return to Earth. The day before, it had been *Shalom Lach Eretz Nehederet*, for Israeli astronaut Ilan Ramon. Thursday morning it had been John Lennon's *Imagine*. *Scotland the Brave* was for mission specialist Laurel Clark, of Scottish heritage.

"Good morning," Mission Control called up to the ship.

"Good morning, Houston," Clark answered. "We're getting ready for our big day up here ... I'm really excited to come back home. Hearing that song reminds me of all the different places down on Earth and all the friends and family that I have all over the world."

She had reason to be excited, particularly since that business of coming home should have been relatively routine, at least by the high-wire standards of space travel. After shimmying out of their sleep restraints, the crew would stow gear and belt themselves into their seats—a process that would take a good six hours. With *Columbia* turned rump forward, the commander would then fire the main maneuvering engines, slowing the spacecraft and easing it toward the upper wisps of the atmosphere. Once he turned the ship around, he would surf the currents of the steadily thickening air, fishtailing this way and that until, just an hour or so after the de-orbit engines were lighted, *Columbia's* tires would make their smoking contact with the Cape Canaveral runway and the shuttle would come to a rolling stop. Welcome home!

That's the way it ought to have happened, at least—and that's the way it did happen on 111 previous shuttle flights, 27 of them by the venerable *Columbia*, America's first shuttle. But only 15 min. from its planned touchdown, more than 200,000 ft. (61,000 m) over Texas, the 22-year-old ship suddenly and fatally deconstructed itself, taking the lives of its seven crew members with it. "A space-shuttle contingency has been declared," the voice of Mission Control intoned in the arid argot of the space agency.

What went wrong? Commander Rick Husband fired his

TEARS FOR A FALLING STAR

Seven astronauts perish when the space shuttle *Columbia* burns up as it re-enters Earth's atmosphere, and NASA's safety procedures are blamed

STREAK: *Columbia*, already in trouble, passes over the Owens Radio Observatory near Bishop, CA

de-orbit engines at 8:15 a.m. E.T. when the ship was high over the Indian Ocean. Half an hour—and half a world—later, it hit the edges of the atmosphere just north of Hawaii at an altitude of about 400,000 ft. (122,000 m). Shortly after, a faint pink glow began to surround the ship, as atmospheric friction caused temperatures to rise to between 750°F and 3,000°F across various parts of the spacecraft's exposed underbelly.

The astronauts, who were busy monitoring their deceleration, temperature, hydraulics and more, didn't have much time to watch the light show play out, and by the time the glow brightened from faint pink to bright pink to plasma white, the ship had arced around the planet into thick air and daylight. "It all happens so smoothly … you hardly notice it," says retired astronaut Henry Hartsfield Jr., who piloted *Columbia* in the early 1980s.

On the ground, things were smooth too. At Cape Canaveral the conditions were perfect for landing, with temperatures in the low 70s and a light breeze blowing, well within NASA's wind limits. The families of some of the seven crew members had already been shown to the runway, assembling for their up-close view of the touchdown. The pit crew that takes custody of the shuttle and shepherds it back into its hangar was standing by to claim *Columbia* as soon as the crowd cleared. At Mission Control in Houston things were similarly routine. "Many of us came in today marveling at the fact that one of the most difficult things we deal with is weather, and we didn't have any weather issues anywhere in the world," said chief flight director Milt Heflin.

The weather would soon seem irrelevant. At 8:53 a.m., when the ship was crossing over San Francisco, a data point flickered on monitors at Mission Control indicating that the flow of information recording the temperature of the hydraulic systems in *Columbia's* left wing had suddenly ceased. At 8:56, when the ship was somewhere over Utah, the temperature in the landing gear and brake lining—again on the left side—registered high. Two minutes later, three temperature sensors embedded in the skin on the left flank of the ship quit transmitting. A minute later, tem-

ALL SMILES: The crew of the *Columbia* lines up for an upbeat in-flight video news conference. From left in the front row, flight surgeon David Brown, mission commander Rick Husband and payload commander Michael Anderson. In the back row, from left, are payload specialist Ilan Ramon, mission specialist Kalpana Chawla, pilot William McCool and mission specialist Laurel Clark. Ramon was Israel's first astronaut; his mother and grandmother are Auschwitz survivors. Chawla, who was born in India, had become a U.S. citizen. More than half the crew aboard the *Columbia* were space-flight rookies

NASA

perature sensors in the left tires winked out too. All these data hiccups were reported by the mission controllers to the flight director. Finally, when the spacecraft was about 207,000 ft. (63,000 m) above Texas, Charlie Hobaugh, the spacecraft communicator, alerted the craft.

"*Columbia*, Houston," he said. "We see your tire-pressure message."

"Roger," Husband responded. "Uh ..." All at once, communications were cut off as if by a knife, and with them went every other scrap of data coming down from the ship.

"*Columbia*, Houston," Hobaugh said. "Com check." Static crackled back. "*Columbia*, Houston. UHF com check," Hobaugh said again, as Mission Control switched channels.

Still no response.

"*Columbia*, Houston," Hobaugh repeated several more times, but still there was nothing. Mission controllers—at least the veterans—did not expect there would be. "We lost all vehicle data," says Heflin. "That's when we began to know that we had a bad day."

Outside Mission Control, in the hot path the flaming *Columbia* cut through the sky, no one needed to see computer data to know the day had taken a bad turn. Outside Nacogdoches, Texas, 17-year-old Heath Drewery was in bed when he was jolted by what sounded like an explosion outside his house. "I heard this big rumble and thought a train had derailed," he says. He and his brother piled into their truck and drove into town, where the street was

LAUNCH: Investigators fingered hardened foam that came loose and struck the left wing of *Columbia* at lift-off on Jan. 16 as the root cause of its incineration

CHRIS O'MEARA—AP/WIDE WORLD

cluttered with debris. "There were pieces all over the place. It looked like it was charcoal." In San Augustine, things got more grisly, when body parts fell from the sky.

With reports coming back of a debris field that stretched from eastern Texas to Louisiana, NASA put out the somewhat disingenuous word that fumes from the fragments could be dangerous and that people who found them should leave them where they lay and alert the authorities—as if any toxic fuel could have survived the heat of re-entry. The more probable reason for the space agency's alerts was that tampering with the debris would make a proper investigation of the disaster that much harder. Worse, within hours scraps purported to be from the lost spacecraft were already being hawked on eBay, the Internet auction site.

At Camp David, President Bush was in his cabin when chief of staff Andrew Card phoned with the news; Bush decided to return to the White House by motorcade. A grim Bush scheduled a conference call with the families for 12:45, and at 12:30 he was standing at his desk in the Oval Office scanning biographies of the crew members to see which ones had spouses and children. "Tough day, tough day," he muttered. After placing the call, he left the office briefly to compose himself. "He was emotional," said a speechwriter who was there. "He was misty eyed."

Even as searchers scoured much of the southern tier of the country for remains of the ship, a second search—for the cause of the crash—began. Images of *Columbia's* demise were sent in by amateur videotapers, and reports of evidence were phoned in by free-lance debris hunters. Part of the leading edge of one wing turned up near Fort Worth, Texas, while a rear-wing section was examined in the eastern part of the state, near Nacogdoches. Researchers dug up old NASA memos warning of just the kind of accident that may have claimed *Columbia*. Experts sought to reassemble 32 seconds of vital, if patchy, data that sputtered down from *Columbia* after the voice communication link was lost.

AS NASA SCRAMBLED TO MANAGE EVENTS, officials in Washington began taking sides, some sharpening the long knives for the agency, others lining up to defend it. "Space exploration will go on," said Senator Mary Landrieu, Democrat of Louisiana. "[But] there will be intense investigations."

Those investigations got under way even before the shuttle debris was cool. In the hours after the crash, suspicions centered on a notorious incident: a bit of hardened foam had fallen from the external fuel tank during the

> ❝ **We lost all vehicle data. That's when we knew we had a bad day.** ❞
>
> —**CHARLIE HOBAUGH, NASA**

Jan. 16 lift-off, striking *Columbia's* left-wing area. Applied like shaving cream, the foam dries to the hardness of a brick, which could conceivably damage the fragile external tiles that protect the shuttle during its fiery re-entry. Indeed, the spacecraft had spent 39 days idling on the pad before launch, enduring episodes of freezing rain that could have loosened the foam further.

Yet other possible reasons for the crash soon emerged, including a theory that the calamity was caused by plasma—superhot gas—leaking into the ship's wheel well. New records revealed that the heat in the left wheel well began to increase when the shuttle was still over the Pacific, heading for California. That suggested the ship sustained damage in orbit but began to feel the effects only when the temperature rose during re-entry.

A direct view of the homebound crew in the moments leading up to the crash was provided when a 13-min. videotape was recovered partly intact from the wreckage. Hauntingly, the tape shows a calm, collected group, with commander Husband, pilot William McCool and crew members Clark and Kalpana Chawla strapped into their seats on the main flight deck. Crewmates Ramon, David Brown and Michael Anderson are out of view, similarly belted into place on the middeck below. The tape runs from 8:35 to 8:48 a.m. E.T.—ending about 11 min.

JIGSAW PUZZLE: NASA is collecting the recovered pieces of the shuttle in a hangar at the Kennedy Space Center in Florida as part of the inquiry into the crash. As of May, when this picture was taken, more than 82,000 pieces had been shipped to Florida, and 78,760 of them had been identified

ELEVONS The rear flaps that control the shuttle's pitch during re-entry were closely studied. There were reports of unusual movements in the elevons before the breakup, and loss of data from sensors in the flaps was one of the first signs that something had gone seriously wrong

LEFT WING Shortly after lift-off on Jan. 16, a piece of the external fuel tank's insulating foam shook loose and struck the left wing, the second such incident in four months. In August, the independent review board established that this incident caused the crash

Oxidizer tanks

Oxidizer tanks

Liquid-hydrogen supply

Commander Rick Husband

Mission specialist Kalpana Chawla

Pilot William McCool

Mission specialist Laurel Blair Salton Clark

Columbia

Payload commander Michael Anderson

Payload specialist Ilan Ramon

Mission spec David Brown

MAIN ENGINES Three main engines operate for about 8.5 minutes during lift-off and ascent. They have no role in re-entry

PAYLOAD This is where equipment for the more than 80 scientific experiments was housed

ORBITER The forward fuselage contains the cockpit, living quarters and computers that control navigation

THE LAST MOMENTS

Heightening the mystery, NASA saw no signs of trouble until a few minutes before the shuttle disintegrated. It had successfully completed a tricky S-turn when mission control noticed a series of strange data readings from sensors in the left wing

4 9 a.m.
Altitude: 207,135 ft. (63,135 m) at a speed of Mach 18.
The shuttle continues gliding in at about 12,500 m.p.h. (20,000 km/h). Within the next several minutes communication and tracking links with NASA are mysteriously cut off. *Columbia* disintegrates over the Dallas–Fort Worth area

1 8:15 a.m. E.T., in space
Traveling at 17,318 m.p.h. (27,870 km/h) at a height of 176 miles (283.2 km) over the Indian Ocean
Given the "go" for deorbit burn, the braking maneuver that sends the shuttle back to earth. The *Columbia* fires its rockets to slow down its speed and descends in a head-first belly-forward position to deflect the heat of re-entry

2 8:56 a.m.
Over California
NASA reports an increase in brakewell and tire temperatures at this point, but assumes they are false readings due to the loss of sensor data. In hindsight, NASA believes the data may have been correct

3 8:59 a.m.
Last full crew transmission to NASA, acknowledging that they had seen measurements citing tire temperatures and pressures

TEXAS

Sources: NASA, Kennedy Space Center, Johnson Space Center, AP

COLUMBIA'S FINAL FLIGHT

Why did the space shuttle *Columbia* self-destruct?
NASA detectives searched for clues in the complex
details of the shuttle's construction and in the
precise sequence of events in the final minutes and
seconds before its catastrophic failure

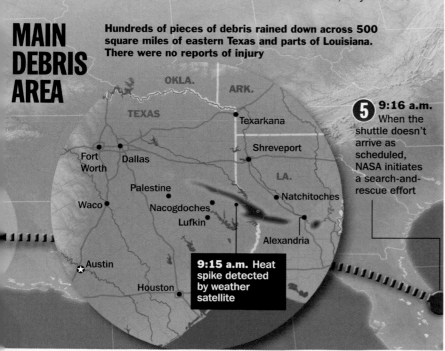

THRUSTERS Used to control the shuttle in space and during re-entry. Investigators looked at their performance and at a possible fuel ignition problem

Emittance coating

Tile body

■ Graphic by Jackson Dykman, Ed Gabel, Joe Lertola and Lon Tweeten. Reported by Missy Adams

Strain isolator pad made of felted fiber

Aluminum structure

THERMAL TILES The 24,000 tiles that protect the shuttle from the soaring temperatures of re-entry have been trouble from the start. The fact that the accident occurred at the point when the vehicle was at its hottest—some 3000°F (1,650°C)—immediately raised the possibility that the tiles were somehow to blame; they were not

MAIN DEBRIS AREA

Hundreds of pieces of debris rained down across 500 square miles of eastern Texas and parts of Louisiana. There were no reports of injury

OKLA.
ARK.
TEXAS
Texarkana
Shreveport
LA.
Fort Worth
Dallas
Palestine
Natchitoches
Waco
Nacogdoches
Lufkin
Alexandria
Austin
Houston

5 **9:16 a.m.** When the shuttle doesn't arrive as scheduled, NASA initiates a search-and-rescue effort

9:15 a.m. Heat spike detected by weather satellite

---

before the ship was destroyed in midair.

Immediately after the accident, NASA announced the formation of an in-house panel to identify the cause of the crash. Critics howled that no agency, particularly not one in such hot water, should be allowed to investigate itself. And after 16 Democratic members of the House wrote a letter of protest to the White House, NASA backed away, ceding the job to an independent 13-person review board, headed by retired U.S. Navy Admiral Harold Gehman.

On Aug. 26, the *Columbia* Accident Investigation Board issued a report that determined the cause of the crash and also dealt a stinging rebuke to the space agency. The report said the piece of foam that had come loose during take-off pierced the shuttle's protective skin. The resulting hole in the wing allowed superhot gases to enter as the shuttle reached the earth's atmosphere, dooming the craft. It went on to charge that NASA managers were "as much a cause" of the tragedy as were technical faults, and highlighted "organizational compromises" and managerial oversights that led NASA to ignore alarm bells.

"We are convinced that the management practices overseeing the Space Shuttle Program were as much a cause of the accident as the foam that struck the left wing," the report said. It claimed that a culture of complacency had crept into the agency, particularly in the all-important area of crew safety. Too few staff, budgetary constraints and dated equipment also contributed to the disaster, the report concluded. It also recommended that NASA set up independent safety teams that would be given direct access to top agency officials.

But Gehman also called NASA an "outstanding organization." And, to the consternation of the growing number of opponents of the shuttle program, the board recommended that flights resume.

NASA Administrator Sean O'Keefe responded to the report by accepting its findings in full—including the charge that the agency's culture was a factor in the accident. He called the panel's conclusions "a blueprint ... a road map" for change at the agency. "It's going to be a long road," he warned. Indeed. But if America's exploration of space is to go on—with the least cost in human lives—that journey will have to be taken. ■

FACING DOWN
A PANDEMIC

Coronaviruses normally cause nothing more serious than a cold, but somehow

A killer coronavirus emerges in China, but fast work by global health workers limits its impact

EARLY APRIL 2003: RESEARCHERS AT THE UNIVERSITY OF Hong Kong's pathology lab gathered around a powerful transmission electron microscope and stared a newly accused mass-murder suspect right in the face. They were investigating a virus unknown to science only a month before, a minuscule particle of protein-encrusted RNA that was almost certainly the microbe that had infected more than 2,400 people in 19 countries—including up to 115 in the U.S.—and killed at least 89 since it began its rampage through the human population in China in the fall of 2002.

Projected onto a green phosphorescent screen by a beam of electrons, the virus particles—taken from a relative of the Chinese doctor who became Hong Kong's first fatality on March 4—looked chillingly like aliens in a sci-fi film. Magnified 100,000 times, the organisms were fuzzy little balls that filled the screen and looked like the burrs that stick to your pants during a hike through the woods. Tiny hooks poked out of the spherical bodies—a telltale characteristic that helped classify the pathogen as a member of the coronavirus family. But while coronaviruses normally cause nothing more serious than a cold, these microbes had evidently, for reasons unknown, mutated into a sometimes deadly infectious agent that would terrify much of the planet in the weeks to come.

The virus was soon given a name: SARS, short for severe acute respiratory syndrome. When news of the first cases of the disease began emerging from mainland China in March, health authorities around the world went on high alert. Such was the level of concern that, for the first time in its 55-year history, the World Health Organization (WHO) recommended that travelers avoid nonessential trips to an entire region—China's Guangdong province and Hong Kong, right next door—for fear that they might contract and further spread the infectious agent.

Why the strong measures? Epidemiologists are haunted by the great Spanish influenza pandemic of 1918-19; it killed fewer than 3% of its victims but infected so many people that at least 20 million people died in just 18 months—more than were killed in combat in World War I. For years, infectious-disease specialists have warned that the world is ripe for the return of just such a pandemic—and the early trajectory of the SARS outbreak fit the pattern.

Fortunately—and experts say it is still too soon to make final pronouncements—the world seems to have averted

CAUTION: Residents of Hong Kong don masks to ward off the SARS virus. Chinese authorities mounted an elaborate campaign to keep the virus outbreak secret late in 2002, but by March 2003 the situation was out of control

ese microbes mutated into a deadly infectious agent that spooked the planet

THE STORY OF SARS BEGINS IN NOVEMBER 2002, when a mysterious respiratory illness began spreading through China's southern province of Guangdong. In the first phase, patients experienced a fever of 100.4°F or more, with chills, headache and muscle aches. Within a week, most victims developed a dry cough and difficulty in breathing; about 10% to 20% required a ventilator. A few also got severe diarrhea. And some—as many as eight individuals of every 100 infected—died.

At this critical moment, China's officials made a grievous error: they kept the outbreak quiet to prevent terror instead of broadcasting its presence and working to contain it. By February 2003, at least 305 Guangdong residents had developed SARS. By the time China finally turned in a two-page report to WHO officials a month later, the disease was on the move.

In early March the illness landed in Hong Kong. Health officials there have become particularly skilled at identifying respiratory diseases because the city is located so near China's rich agricultural zones, where pigs, poultry and millions of people live in close proximity. Illnesses like influenza routinely jump from animals to humans, which is why new strains of flu often originate in Asia.

Alert to the fact that something strange was going on, authorities in Hong Kong quickly notified WHO; its officials immediately issued an unprecedented global alert, clamped down on travel into and out of Hong Kong, and, along with the U.S. Centers for Disease Control and Prevention and labs in other nations,

an outbreak that might have proved just as deadly as that of 1918-19. Still, before the SARS epidemic was brought under control, it carved a path of illness, death and economic calamity that highlighted the vulnerability of the modern world to the sudden appearance of a completely new virus. It taught other lessons, as well. Early attempts by the Chinese government to hush up news of the disease underlined the necessity of dealing with such problems swiftly and in full public view, for the attempt to avert panic only gave the virus time to spread. On the positive side of the ledger, the containment of SARS was a tribute to the decisive and swift actions of the worldwide health community, which treated the potential pandemic with a combination of scientific detective work, global cooperation and stern public health measures that may have saved tens of thousands of lives—and perhaps far more.

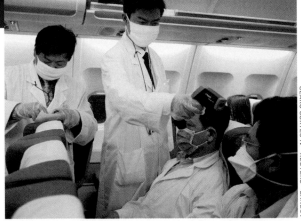

WARY: At top left, choirboys are masked at a Hong Kong cathedral on Good Friday. Above, passengers traveling from Hong Kong to Shangai's Pudong International Airport early in May are tested for fever before being allowed to deplane

In the last great pandemic, the Spanish influenza outbreak of 1918-19, following

launched an impressively coordinated effort to understand the illness—fast. Pathologists at the University of Hong Kong soon identified a probable culprit: a mutated coronavirus, one of a common, generally not severe family of viruses.

But SARS didn't stop in Hong Kong; by mid-March people were dying of the disease in faraway Toronto. Officials later traced the outbreak to an elderly Canadian couple of Chinese descent who had flown in after a Hong Kong vacation, setting off a chain reaction that would infect 138 Ontario residents, leave a total of 20 dead and force more than 10,000 people into quarantine over a four-week period.

By May 1, WHO had tallied more than 4,800 cases in at least 26 countries; some 300 people had died. The disease had rocked Asian markets, ruined the tourist trade of China and Hong Kong and landed Toronto on an official WHO do-not-visit list. The U.S. was fortunate: only about 40 people contracted the disease, and none died from it.

Early May also brought progress in decoding the virus; scientists at the School of Medicine at Washington University in St. Louis succeeded in sequencing the SARS genome, a key step in developing a vaccine to stop it.

Indeed, SARS proved tough to stop. In Toronto, officials eager to remove themselves from under the illness's taint thought they had their outbreak under control in late April, but in June they confronted a second flurry of some 100 infections that was traced to a single floor of a Toronto hospital. The city was not released from the travel advisory until mid-summer; officials estimated Canada's economy had taken a $400 million hit from the episode.

One factor of SARS scientists found baffling is the superspreader, a person who appears to pass the disease on with extraordinary efficiency. Part of the explanation may be in the individual's genetics. "We don't know what those genetic factors are yet, " said Dr. Anthony Fauci, director of the National Institute of Allergy and Infectious Diseases in late May, "But they're not neccessarily related to how sick the person is." Some experts suspect that superspreaders might have a more virulent strain of coronavirus or be coinfected with other microbes. Having multiple infections may, the scientist speculate, increase one's chance of passing on the disease.

By the fall of 2003, all was quiet on the SARS front. The epidemic appeared to be contained—for the short run. But too many loose ends remained: there is still no fast, reliable diagnostic test, and WHO estimates there will be no SARS vaccine until 2006. Researchers hoped to develop a test by early 2004, in time for the winter flu season, just when they feared the disease might return, possibly in a more virulent form. A key concern: the virus did not weaken as it passed through the human population, as officials had hoped it would. Worse, the virus seems to mutate rapidly, increasing the likelihood that a nasty new variant could appear. Yes, much of the world dodged the SARS bullet in 2003—but watch out for the ricochet. ∎

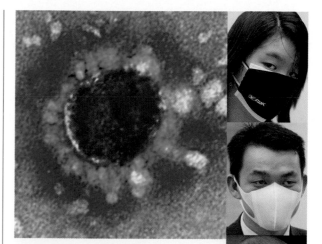

■ SARS: A BRIEFING

WHAT IT IS
SARS (severe acute respiratory syndrome) is a respiratory illness that primarily affects the lungs but may also involve the digestive tract.

THE SYMPTOMS
In the first phase, patients get a fever of 100.4°F or more, usually with chills, headache and muscle aches. Within a week, most develop a dry cough and difficulty in breathing; about 10% to 20% require a ventilator. Some also get severe diarrhea. About 8% of those infected die.

THE CAUSE
Coronaviruses often infect animals and until now have caused only mild illness in people; they are responsible for the common cold. It may turn out that SARS results from simultaneous infection by several microbes.

HOW THE VIRUS SPREADS
The most common route is direct person-to-person contact. Unlike influenza or tuberculosis, SARS is transmitted not through the air but most likely by droplets spread when an infected person coughs or sneezes.

TREATMENT
There is still no cure. Patients are given supportive care for their symptoms, such as ventilators to aid breathing and fluids to prevent deyhdration. Researchers are trying to develop a vaccine, which is not expected to be ready until 2006. The good news: scientists have already sequenced the entire genome of the coronavirus, a major step in understanding the disease and developing better treatments.

Vorld War I, more people died from the disease than were killed on the battlefield

PRESCRIPTIONS FOR WELL-BEING

The health beat covers some unexpected ground, from pocket pets and pasta to "pharmaceuticals" and pitcher's mounds. The bad news: after 30 years, we're still debating whether we should eat more pasta and less steak—or vice versa. The good news: dark chocolate is good for you!

ELSA—GETTY IMAGES

GEORGE MATTEI—ENVISION FOR TIME

DARK CHOCOLATE
A small study done in Germany indicated that dark chocolate may be good for your heart. The sweet contains polyphenols, which reduce blood pressure in animals; it also declined in the German test on humans. The downside? Sorry, we couldn't find one!

EPHEDRA
This over-the-counter supplement is similar to an amphetamine; it's used by many people to control appetite and by athletes to gain energy. The substance has been implicated in the deaths of baseball pitchers Steven Bechler and Darryl Kile, above. In 2003, U.S. health officials required that ephedra include a label warning it may be harmful.

FARMACEUTICALS
Cures on the cob? Don't laugh. Biotech companies are using the data in the map of the human genome to create all manner of plant-based pharmaceuticals. Researchers have launched more than 300 trials of genetically engineered crops to produce everything from fruit-based hepatitis vaccines to AIDS drugs grown in tobacco leaves. They call the process biopharming. Critics—and there are many—call it Pharmageddon. What's behind the revolution? Cost. Growing drugs in plants could cut production expenses in half.

MIKE ROEMER—GETTY IMAGES

MONKEYPOX VIRUS
An outbreak of monkeypox, the first ever in the western hemisphere, afflicted more than 60 Midwesterners in the spring. Health officials traced the outbreak to 28 prairie dogs in Wisconsin, so-called pocket pets, that had been infected by a giant Gambian pouched rat while in transit.The U.S. banned the importation of rodents from Africa and stopped prairie dog sales.

CONJOINED TWINS
New surgical methods are allowing doctors to explore the unlinking of conjoined twins, a procedure that had seldom been attempted before recent years. Two such attempts were in the news in 2003: in the first, a pair of 29-year-old Iranian twins, Ladan and Laleh Bijani, underwent a 50-hour operation in Singapore. Both twins died. In a happier result, a pair of two-year-old Egyptian twins joined at the head were successfully separated by doctors at a hospital in Dallas.

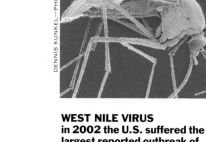

WEST NILE VIRUS
in 2002 the U.S. suffered the largest reported outbreak of West Nile virus in the world, with 4,156 infections and 284 deaths. Early in 2003, U.S. health officials warned that the year's toll from the mosquito-borne disease could be much worse. By fall, when the mosquito season was over, many more cases had been reported—8,393—but the number of deaths had declined to 184.

LOW-CARB DIETS
More and more people are signing on to the diet plan advocated by nutritionist Robert Atkins, who died early in 2003. The plan calls for a diet low in carbo-hydrates, like bread, pasta and milk, and high in such protein-rich foods as butter, eggs and meat. Two 2003 studies argued for the Atkins plan. One found that after six months, subjects who followed a low-carb diet lost at least twice as much weight as those on a high-carb, low-fat diet. And both showed that the low-carb diet boosted the levels of HDL, the good cho-lesterol, while lowering the amount of the potentially dangerous fats called triglycerides.

Nutrition Fac[

Serving Size 1 cup (228g)
Servings Per Container 2

Amount Per Serving

Calories 260	Calories from Fat 120

	% Daily Value*
Total Fat 13g	**20%**
Saturated Fat 5g	**25%**
Trans Fat 2g	
Cholesterol 30mg	**10%**
Sodium 660mg	**28%**
Total Carbohydrate 31g	**10%**
Dietary Fiber 0g	**0%**
Sugars 5g	
Protein 5g	

Vitamin A 4%	●	Vitamin C 2%
Calcium 15%	●	Iron 4%

* Percent Daily Values are based on a 2,000 calorie diet. Your Daily Values may be higher or lower depending on your calorie needs:

	Calories:	2,000	2,500
Total Fat	Less than	65g	80g
Sat Fat	Less than	20g	25g
Cholesterol	Less than	300mg	300mg
Sodium	Less than	2,400mg	2,400mg
Total Carbohydrate		300g	375g
Dietary Fiber		25g	30g

Calories per gram:
Fat 9   *   Carbohydrates 4   *   Protein 4

TRANS FATS
On July 9, 2003, the FDA declared that in 2006 it would begin requiring food labels to include the amount of trans-fatty acids in a product. Created when hydrogen is added to vegetable oil, trans fats raise the level of bad cholesterol, may lower the rate of good cholesterol and are believed to be as destructive to arteries as saturated fat, perhaps even more so. Widely used, the fats can be found in cookies, vegetable shortening, crackers, French fries and puddings. Look for the phrase "contains partially hydrogenated vegetable oil."

HERO: Chinese space-agency workers give pioneer Yang a lift after his landing

■ PROFILE

Nefertiti Found?

A team of scientists working in Egypt in 2003 emerged with what they claim are compelling clues that a stripped and mutilated mummy, first discovered in a side chamber of a royal tomb more than 100 years ago, is Nefertiti, the glamorous young queen who died some 3,300 years ago. The celebrated beauty was married, perhaps as young as age 12, to the Pharaoh Amenhotep, who abolished Egypt's polytheistic system in favor of a religion based on worshipping the sun god, Aten; he even took the name Akhenaten.

MYSTERY: Is this vandalized mummy Nefertiti?

Nefertiti vanished from history after the 12th year of her husband's reign, and the tomb where she and Akhenaten were laid was later sacked. But in 1898, when archaeologists opened another royal tomb, the remains of several Pharaohs were found within, as well as three stripped mummies. One of them, a middle-age woman, had her head shaved, the style favored by Nefertiti. Further clues—a pierced earlobe, the impression of a royal headband and the high quality of the embalming—suggest but do not prove that the mummy may be that of Akhenaten's wife.

Red Sky at Morning

Welcome a new nation to the exploration of space: China's Long March-II-F rocket launched *taikonaut* Yang Liwei into orbit around Earth on Oct. 15. Yang completed 14 orbits, staying aloft for 21 hours before his *Shenzou 5* (Divine Vessel 5) spacecraft touched down on the grasslands of Mongolia. China's leaders and people hailed Yang as a hero. But fans of urban legends were saddened when he reported, "The scenery was very beautiful. But I did not see the Great Wall."

Mapping the Big Bang

Since July 2001, the Wilkinson Microwave Anisotropy Probe, or WMAP, has been orbiting in deep space, a million miles from Earth, studying the most ancient light in existence. Its findings, released early in 2003, offer a new map of the echoes of the Big Bang. The news: the universe is 13.7 billion years old, and the first stars blinked on 200 million years after the Big Bang. The universe is made up of three things: 4% ordinary atoms; 23% "dark matter," whose nature is still unknown; and 73% "dark energy," the mysterious force whose antigravity effect is speeding up cosmic expansion. Cosmologists

COBE

WMAP

NEW VIEW: Top, a 1992 map of Big Bang echoes; below, the 2003 map

said the results will put their science on a factual rather than speculative basis for the first time.

A Jurassic Glider

Fossils of a four-winged species of dinosaur discovered in China provide further evidence for those paleontologists who argue that birds, which are believed to have evolved from dinosaurs, took their first flight gliding down from trees, rather than from the ground up, as some theories maintain. *Microraptor gui*, about 3 ft. long from head to tail, died out 128 million years ago.

Images

Sharks Lost?
Many species of the sea's apex predator are at risk, even more so than we'd realized. A team that examined the logbooks of U.S. fishing boats in the northwestern Atlantic from 1986 to 2000 found almost all shark species have declined 50%. The problem: the big fish are eaten as delicacies; trophy-hunted; and snagged in longlines, cables as long as 20 miles and studded with up to 500 baited hooks.

HENRY WALCOTT—AP/WIDE WORLD

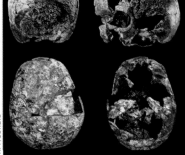

AFP/CORBIS

FIRST MAN? The three new skulls

The 160,000-Year-Old Man

Three skulls unearthed in Ethiopia in 1997 may offer our first look at the earliest true *Homo sapiens*—older by at least 1,000 generations than any fossils previously found. The specimens, said the University of California's Tim White, co-chief of the research team that found them, prove that there were anatomically modern humans in Africa long before there were classic Neanderthals in Europe, indicating that the Neanderthals were a side branch on the human evolutionary tree that died out. White's team also said the fossils prove that the first humans emigrated from Africa and then spread around the world, rather than arising simultaneously in several areas, as proponents of the theory of multiregionalism believe. One mystery: the skulls had been handled, even polished, after death. Ruling out cannibalism, the scientists pondered whether early man may have had mortuary rites.

Ready for Its Close-Up

Mars, our closest planetary neighbor, has proved less than neighborly to earthly visitors. Of the 33 missions to the Red Planet since 1960, 22 probes have crashed, broken up en route or otherwise failed before they reached the planet. But in 2003, as Mars made its nearest approach to our planet in 60,000 years, undaunted earthlings launched yet another assault on Mars. In June, three spacecraft—two from NASA, one from the European Space Agency—took flight. The missions, if successful, could go a long way toward explaining the history, geology and biology of mysterious Mars.

The two U.S. craft will each release on the surface a remote-controlled rover that is bigger, smarter and better equipped than the miniature marvel that was the hero of the 1997 Pathfinder voyage. The European mission includes an orbiter and a lander that carries a drill, plus 12 ovens to heat samples and identify their chemistry.

NASA

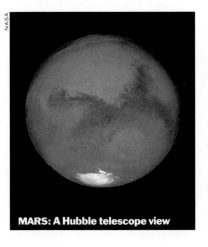

MARS: A Hubble telescope view

Diva Las Vegas

It was a marriage made in NAFTA heaven: Canada's over-the-top belter and America's over-the-top city. And since this is Las Vegas, we'll skip the music and get straight to the numbers. To lure Celine Dion to the Strip, Caesars Palace hotel and casino erected a $95 million, 4,000-seat theater, with a private elevator for Dion's use; a below-stage, eight-room suite reserved for her family; and a $2 million atmospheric bubble to keep the onstage humidity at a constant 55%. She will perform her Cirque du Soleil–style show, *A New Day*, some 200 nights a year for three years. Her take: a reported $100 million plus 50% of the profits. Your ante: $87.50 to $200 a ticket.

The Arts

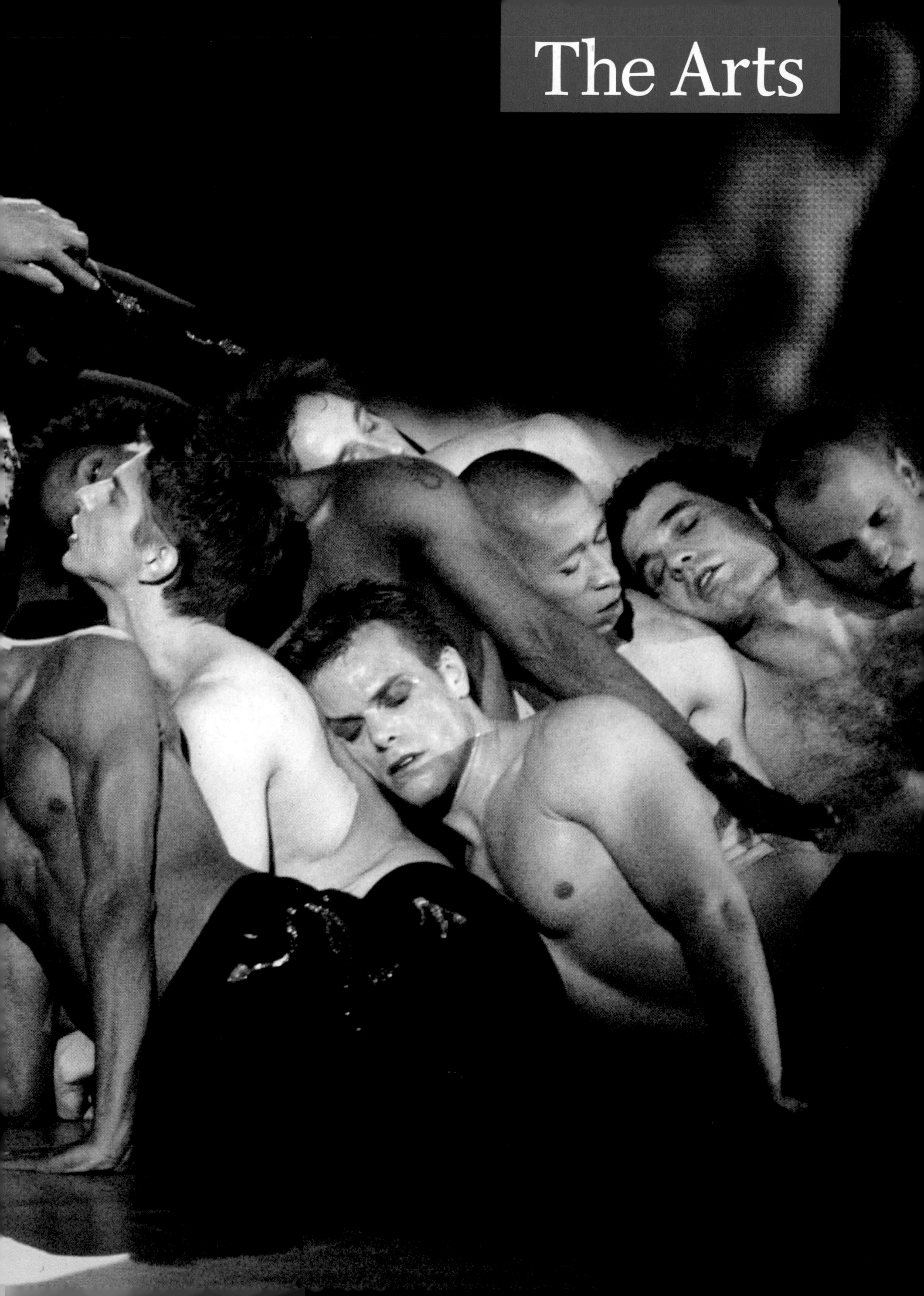

AMERICAN IDOL

PALS: Clay Aiken, left, finished second to Ruben Stoddard, right, on *American Idol*, but both singers seemed to have promising futures

■ Sure, reality TV is tawdry, dirty and cheap—that's why we love it. New in 2003:

THE RESTAURANT

JOE MILLIONAIRE

GUILTY PLEASURES

We say we hate reality TV, but we sure seem to watch a lot of it. Maybe that's because it makes us part of a communal experience

REALITY TV IS THE ONE MASS-ENTERTAINMENT CATE-gory that thrives because of its audience's contempt for it. Sure, it makes us feel tawdry, dirty, cheap—if it didn't, we probably wouldn't bother tuning in. And in 2003 we were tuning in, by the millions, to such fare as *Joe Millionaire, The Bachelorette* and *American Idol.* To paraphrase Winston Churchill, never have so many watched so much TV with so little good to say about it. Yet it's entirely possible the reality craze has been good for television. It has given the networks water-cooler buzz again; it has reminded viewers jaded by sitcoms and dramas why TV can be exciting; and at its best, it is teaching TV a new way to tell involving human stories. Reality shows don't just reach tens of millions of viewers but leave them feeling part of a communal experience—what network TV does best. (Of course, the genre also offers plenty of dismal, crass, indefensible shows—but, hey, that's TV.)

The new network shows for fall 2003 were a creatively timid mass of remakes, bland family comedies and derivative cop dramas. Network executives dubbed them "comfort"—i.e., familiar and boring—TV. Whereas reality TV—call it "discomfort TV"—lives to rattle viewers' cages. It provokes. It offends. But at least it's trying to do something besides help you get to sleep.

Fox's *American Idol* continued to set the pace for reality shows in 2003; more than 33 million people tuned in on May 21 to see the appealing crooner Ruben Stoddard voted the show's top performer over the, uh, appealing croon-er Clay Aiken. The show's clout later reverberated on the pop-music charts, when Aiken's CD *Measure of a Man* sold 613,000 units in its first week—the biggest first-week seller since 1993. Worshipping at *Idol's* shrine were a raft of spin-offs: USA network's *Nashville Star,* CBS's *Star Search,* ABC's *All-American Girl,* even Animal Planet's *Pet Star.*

Let a thousand romance shows bloom! On Fox's *Joe Millionaire,* 20 women convened at a château in France to compete for Evan Marriott, a tree trunk of a man who had inherited $50 million—or so the women were told. In truth, he was a construction worker earning $19,000 a year. On ABC's *The Bachelorette,* 25 men gathered in Los Angeles to vie for Trista Rehn, an also-ran from the first season of *The Bachelor.* Makeover shows also prospered; the clever twist on this staple of the women's magazine genre was Bravo's *Queer Eye for the Straight Guy,* which set five hyperactive gay men to the task of transforming woebegone heterosexual ducks into hip metrosexual swans.

When all else failed, TV present feasted on the carcass of TV past. Out they came, a parade of the B-list celebs—former child star Emmanuel Lewis, former rapper M.C. Hammer, former Mötley Crüe drummer Vince Neil, former sitcom star Kathy Griffin—a harvest of has-beens. The genre's omnivorous maw remains unsated: cameras turned up at a New York City restaurant (*The Restaurant,* NBC), at semi-real political huddles (*K Street,* HBO) and in the clanging shops of car customizers (*Monster Garage,* Discovery Channel). Try sleeping over that. ■

dozens of dating shows, talent searches, makeover dramas and other voyeurfests ■

QUEER EYE FOR THE STRAIGHT GUY

MONSTER GARAGE

SLINKY: Frank Gehry's Walt Disney Concert Hall, the new home of the Los Angeles Philharmonic, is intended to help create a vital center for the famously sprawling city of freeways

FORMS OF THE FUTURE

Two inspired buildings offer fresh ways to explore music and art

COZY: Gehry, left, said of the interior of the auditorium, "I wanted to give [visitors] a handrail, a visual handrail." The result—in contrast to the concert hall's unsettling, vertiginous exterior—is a symmetrical space of homey Douglas fir with a floral carpet

THE SILVERY CASCADES OF THE MULTIPLE FAÇADES OF the new Walt Disney Concert Hall in Los Angeles are one of the most beautiful sights anywhere in the U.S. They rival the spectacular Grand Canyon, another sun-drenched, curvy thing of hypnotic power, in their immensity and beauty. Behind this man-made marvel is architect Frank Gehry, whose 1997 masterpiece, the Bilbao Guggenheim Museum in Spain, convinced a thousand cultural organizations that great architecture could draw crowds.

A surprise gift of $50 million by Walt Disney's widow Lillian in 1987 provided the initial funds to build a new home for the Los Angeles Philharmonic, which for years had been unhappily stashed in the Dorothy Chandler Pavilion, a slab of '60s-style bureaucratic neoclassicism with mediocre acoustics. The following year Gehry won the competition to design the new hall. At the time, he was unknown to the general public, and was primarily known among architects and critics for transforming chain link and plywood into respectable building materials.

Meanwhile, plans for the new building lagged. The 1990s was a dark era in Los Angeles, a time of riots, earthquake and recession. Then Gehry's Bilbao museum opened. As Esa-Pekka Salonen, the musical director of the Philharmonic, pointed out, "Frank became this international superstar … and if ever there was a town that understands celebrity, it's L.A." Ground was broken for the new building in 1999.

Within the building's slip-sliding-away exterior, Gehry designed a warm, symmetrical interior in cozy Douglas fir, with gentle curves that strongly recall the work of Alvar Aalto, the Finnish architect whose work is one of Gehry's lifelong inspirations. Gehry's multicolored floral-pattern upholstery is a nod to the comfort factor and a tribute to Lillian

VOIDS: Michael Heizer's *North, East, South, West*, (1957-1962) is a series of geometric Cor-Ten steel holes, 20 ft. deep, embedded into the concrete gallery floor. Dia: Beacon is one of the few galleries large enough to show it

Disney's love of flowers. "I didn't want to create a pseudo-classical hall for classical music," said Gehry. What he has created is a classical hall for an anticlassical city.

L OS ANGELES ISN'T THE ONLY PLACE WHERE PEOPLE THINK big. Over the past three decades, the Dia Art Foundation has spent millions of dollars commissioning and maintaining art, some of it having the dimensions of an Army Corps of Engineers project. In the late 1970s, Dia bought artist Donald Judd a derelict, 340-acre Army post in Marfa, Texas. Judd filled it mostly with his rows of concrete, wood or aluminum boxes. In 1977 Dia paid for and still superintends *The Lightning Field* by Walter De Maria, 400 stainless-steel poles arrayed in a rectangular grid in the desert of New Mexico: width, 1 km; length, 1 mile.

So it was no surprise that when the institution's new outpost, Dia: Beacon, opened in a struggling Hudson River town in upstate New York, it was billed as the world's largest museum of contemporary art. Five years before, Dia director Michael Govan went searching for a building to hold some of the foundation's nearly 700 works. In Beacon

OVERBEARING: Inspired by a Roman church, sculptor Richard Serra designed *Torqued Ellipses* (1996-97) using computer software and had it fabricated at a shipyard. The work's two rolled-steel plates are each 2 in. thick and weigh 20 tons

he found an abandoned factory, built in 1929 and used for decades to print boxes for Nabisco crackers. Fifty million dollars later, the structure is nearly 250,000 sq. ft. of sunlit display space. And much of it will be given over to some of the iciest, most refractory art ever produced—Judd's boxes, Joseph Beuys' piles of felt, Robert Ryman's all-white paintings, Dan Flavin's deliberately plain arrays of fluorescent light tubes.

Dia: Beacon was conceived to present difficult work for long durations. And for much of what it offers, difficult is the word. Dia has what you can only describe as faith in De Maria. For his *Equal Area Series*, 1976-77, the museum is devoting two galleries the length of football fields. At intervals along the floor is a polished steel circle next to a polished steel square, different shapes, but each encompassing an equal area: 25 pairs in all.

Dia also has the space to present some of the weightiest and most forceful postwar American art. The sheer tonnage of Richard Serra's *Torqued Ellipses*, 1996-97, or Michael Heizer's *North, East, South, West*, 1967-2002—four massive

MENACE: *Spider* (1997), one of the huge metal arthropods created by the 87-year-old sculptor Louise Bourgeois in recent years, lurks in an uncomfortable lair at the new Dia gallery. Scary? The artist says the works recall her mother

holes, each a slightly vertiginous 20 ft. deep—operates by pressing down into your nerve paths the heft, the lethal power of the physical world.

Upstairs at Dia is what can only be called the lair of Louise Bourgeois, who inhabits the space like a crazy old aunt in the attic. Born in 1911, Bourgeois is one of the founding figures of feminist art; her sculptural pieces find their sources in the clammiest corners of the psyche and in the meat and moisture of the human body. In recent years she has been showing variations on an enormous metal spider. The one at Dia: Beacon, wedged into a brick-lined confinement, holds in its grip a cage in which you see tattered tapestries that recall the ones Bourgeois's family repaired as a business.

Taken as a pair, Gehry's silvery, soaring concert hall in L.A. and the Dia's massive, industrial-age museum open a new bicoastal dialogue, one whose conflicting visions of a 21st century aesthetic meet and collide, buzzing, somewhere over midcontinent—say, in Marfa, Texas. ∎

Down to the Sea in Sequels

As two celebrated trilogies come to an end, movie screens go maritime

AVAST THERE, MATEY! BUCKLE UP YOUR SWASH, FOR Hollywood has rediscovered a lost genre, the high-seas adventure yarn. The nautical craze began in March 2003, when Pixar, the trailblazing creator of the computer-animated classics *Toy Story* and *Monsters, Inc.*, released *Finding Nemo*, an imaginative undersea adventure that became one of the highest-grossing movies in Hollywood history. In June producer Jerry Bruckheimer's *Pirates of the Caribbean* became the first successful pirate movie since ... well, we can't remember when. In Novem-ber, Aussie Russell Crowe set sail as Captain Jack Aubrey in *Master and Commander: The Far Side of the World*, the first of what promises to be several films based on Patrick O'Brian's learned novels of British naval life. How do we know? Because 2003 also brought the success of the conclusions to the *Lord of the Rings* and *Matrix* series—as well as the second films in the *X-Files* and *Charlie's Angels* series—demonstrating once again the enormous drawing power of the sequel. So batten down the hatches and secure the popcorn: it's anchors aweigh—again! ■

MASTER AND COMMANDER

When Oscar winner Russell Crowe signed on to play the role of Jack Aubrey, he hoped to be wearing out several sets of uniforms—there are 20 volumes in the much loved Patrick O'Brian series. The critics cheered Peter Weir's sea story, but will the box-office take—less than $50 million in the first two weeks—command a sequel?

THE MATRIX

The Brothers Wachowski returned to the dark digital world that enthralled moviegoers in 1999. The big idea: releasing two sequels in a single year, *The Matrix Reloaded* and *The Matrix Revolutions*. Fans were less than enchanted this time, but moguls approved the films' combined box-office take: more than $1 billion.

FINDING NEMO

Pixar's computer wizards worked overtime on this sprightly Bambi-in-the-brine saga, but it may have been the clever screenplay that kept parents and kids returning for second and third viewings. This charming fable, released by Disney, is the highest-grossing animated film in history, topping the studio's *The Lion King*.

THE RETURN OF THE KING

Part three of *The Lord of the Rings* series hit screens in December, bringing director Peter Jackson's lovingly detailed cinematic version of J.R.R. Tolkien's fantasy masterpiece to a triumphant finale. Hollywood insiders were betting that Jackson would receive the Best Picture Oscar for his epic achievement.

■ PROFILE

Curiouser and Curiouser

Matthew Barney may be to Vaseline what Michelangelo was to Carrara marble: Barney piled it, molded it and channeled it down the ramps of the Guggenheim Museum in New York City, where his one-man show in the spring of '03 drew enormous crowds. Barney, 36, primarily a sculptor and filmmaker, has been hailed as the great hope of the art world for more than a decade now; his five-part series of *Cremaster*

BARNEY: Made up in *Cremaster 4*

films are exercises in surrealism that offer lustrous, fascinating episodes amid stretches of state-of-the-art boredom. The five films run for a total of seven hours and contain almost no dialogue. Sample: *Cremaster 3* features a demolition derby in which four sedans smash up a vintage roadster in the lobby of New York City's Chrysler Building.

In the largest show ever for the former high school football player from Boise, Idaho, the Guggenheim's spiraling interior was made over into a recondite theme-park pavilion filled with banners, video screens, Barney's sculptures (he also works in beaver felt and cast tapioca) and other artifacts of the *Cremaster* series, which played nonstop in the museum auditorium.

ROWLING: Beseiged at a book signing by legions of wannabe wizards and witches

Hog Wild for Hogwarts

The story continues … and continues … and continues … for 870 pages, packed with sorcery, Muggles and Quidditch. But that was good news for fans of a certain student at the fictional Hogwarts School of Witchcraft and Wizardry; as they see it, the more the Harry-er. On June 21, in time for the summer solstice, J.K. Rowling's new novel, *Harry Potter and the Order of the Phoenix*, the fifth in the series, went on sale worldwide. The book conjured up statistics as well as spells: at 8.5 million copies, it was the largest first printing of a novel ever. Rowling's fortune is estimated at $450 million, $50 million more than that of the Queen of England.

Yipes! White Stripes!

Basic rock? The music doesn't come much more basic than that

THE WHITES: Related, sort of

offered by rock's White Stripes. The Detroit-based outfit has a cast of two: singer and guitarist Jack White and his "sister" (in reality his ex-wife) Meg White, who handles the drum kit. Their look is as stripped down as their roots-based sound: it

SPRINGER: No such thing as bad publicity

was big news for fans when the duo added a third color, red, to their longtime palette of black and white. *Elephant*, their fourth CD, featured Jack's strong vocals over grinding guitar classics about postbreakup frustration. Purists may have winced to hear a few bass chords and organ fills thrown in, but *Elephant* featured minimalist rock with maximalist thrust.

Springer Meets Wagner

One of the hottest tickets of the 2003 theater season in London offered transsexuals, crude insults, family feuds, a chorus of Ku Klux Klansmen and assorted white-trash yahoos willing to air their tawdriest laundry in public for a few minutes

Images

Homeward Bound
Rekindling the spirit of their popular 1968 song *Old Friends*, Paul Simon and Art Garfunkel reunited for a sold-out series of concerts. The folk-rock pioneers, who had played together infrequently in recent decades, dished up favorite oldies—including the Everly Brothers. Don and Phil offered a few of their classic harmony numbers in the middle of each show, then were joined by their hosts to create a truly Fab Four.

of TV fame. Sound familiar? Brace yourself for *Jerry Springer—The Opera.* The show, with faux operatic music and raunchy lyrics by Richard Thomas and Stewart Lee, was a huge hit at the National Theatre in the spring and transferred to the West End in the fall. Next stop? The producers are aiming for Broadway.

JACKMAN: A Down Under talent is tops in NYC

A Star Is Born

Well, Hugh Jackman has been a star on film since he first donned the long fingernails of Wolverine in the popular series of *X-Men* films. But even though the political success of a certain Austrian-born Californian proved that fans were open to all sorts of extracurricular ambitions in action heroes, singing 20 songs onstage in loud shirts while dancing was probably not among them. Yet when Jackman debuted on Broadway in *The Boy From Oz*, playing Peter Allen, a fellow Aussie who rocketed to fame as a songwriter and singer in the '80s before his death from AIDS in 1992, critics and audiences were dazzled. Jackman, 35, who'd given earlier notice of his power onstage in an acclaimed 1998 London production of *Oklahoma!*, was hailed as a star unequaled on Broadway since the heyday of Ethel Merman and George M. Cohan. The show, however, was panned as a bathetic, by-the-numbers biography of the charismatic Allen, who was mentored early in his career by Judy Garland and—despite being weapons-grade gay—married her daughter Liza Minnelli.

The Last Vexation of Mel

Months before its release, slated for Feb. 25, 2004, Mel Gibson's film *The Passion of Christ* was creating a stir. The film is a realistic account of the last days of Jesus Christ; director Gibson, a Roman Catholic traditionalist, got into hot water with Jews, fellow Catholics and religious scholars, who reacted to early screenings by damning the film as anti-Semitic.

GIBSON: The director, bottom, caused an outcry

Milestones

... Memories

At the risk of sounding macabre, it must be said that 2003 was a very good year for the obituary writers of the world. As living legends passed from the scene, the mind's newsreel unspooled with images: Bob Hope cracking wise; Kate Hepburn one-upping Spencer Tracy; Johnny Cash bearing witness; Daniel Patrick Moynihan arguing a point, eyes dancing with glee; Madame Chiang Kai-shek ... well, Madame Chiang Kai-shek-ing. All together now: Thanks for the ...

**Photograph by
Philippe Halsman**

GRUNTS' FRIEND: Hope entertains U.S. troops in Vietnam, 1968. His pro-war stance would put him out of favor with many younger fans

1903-2003

The Calculating Comic with a Heart of Gold
Gallant trouper and soldiers' joy, Bob Hope leaves behind a million memories

WHEN BOB HOPE DIED AT THE AGE OF 100 ON JULY 27, 2003, it had been 60 years since he made the first of his two appearances on the cover of TIME. That 1943 cover story was prompted by Hope's smashing series of appearances before U.S. and Allied troops stationed in Europe and North Africa in this critical year of World War II. Because the article captures Hope's enduring persona at the moment of its creation, it is worth quoting at length:

"For fighting men," TIME said, "this grimmest of wars is in one small way also the gayest. Never before have the folks who entertain the boys been so numerous or so notable; never have they worked so hard, traveled so far, risked so much … From the ranks of show business have sprung heroes and even martyrs, but so far only one legend. That legend is Bob Hope. It sprang up swiftly, telepathically, among U.S. servicemen in Britain this summer, traveling faster than even whirlwind Hope himself, then flew ahead of him to North Africa and Sicily, growing larger as it went … Hope was funny, treat-

disposable jokes at an industrial pace. The man in the spot-light was supported by an impressive rear echelon: a large team of hard-working writers; advancemen to ferret out local references that could be machine-tooled into laughs; and a vast file of jokes, which he stored in a fireproof vault.

Leslie Towns Hope was born in Eltham England; his father brought his large family to the U.S. when Hope was 4. For-saking his British moniker for the breezier Bob, the youngster worked as a golf caddy, boxed as a professional under the name Packy East, then drifted into vaudeville in a song-and-dance team. But he soon discovered his real gift was for tel-ling jokes. From vaudeville to Broadway, radio to the movies, television to the Internet, Hope kept telling them, famously mastering every major medium of the century.

Vaudeville was the tintype: throughout his career, there was the sense that Hope had just dropped in to share a few topical gags before their due date expired, and soon would be off to the next town—or next radio show, movie or USO show. Even in his films—Hope had a 12-year run in the top 10 at the movie box office—he didn't bother acting; he played Bob

THE ROAD TO IMMORTALITY: An immigrant from Britain, Hope grew up poor, but stardom made him one of Hollywood's wealthiest citizens. He started in show biz as a touring hoofer with partner Lloyd Durbin, left. His NBC show for Pepsodent made him a star in radio's greatest era; he later ruled the screen with Dorothy Lamour and Bing Crosby in seven nutty *Road* films

ing hordes of soldiers to roars of laughter. He was friendly—ate with servicemen, drank with them, read their doggerel, lis-tened to their songs. He was indefatigable, running himself ragged with five, six, seven shows a day. He was figurative—the straight link with home, the radio voice that for years had filled the living room and that in foreign parts called up its im-age. Hence boys whom Hope might entertain for an hour awaited him for weeks. And when he came, anonymous guys who had no other recognition felt personally remembered."

Bob Hope had no special trick of speech, no famous alter ego; he commanded a kind of strenuous averageness. He ba-sically did nothing but stand at a microphone and tell jokes. He was a wiseguy, a smart aleck, a comic minimalist in pur-suit of the perfect gag. He was the comedian for the age of the production line, churning out interchangeable, immediately

Hope. The seven fun *Road* movies he made with another easy-going charmer, Bing Crosby, were excuses to flaunt their per-sonas. Today the films seem surprisingly postmodern in their constant self-reference, as Bing and Bob violate the fourth wall of the screen to comment on, say, how bad that last gag was.

In the 1960s, as society and its comics changed, Hope be-gan to seem old-fashioned. The younger, hipper crowd wanted more bite than Hope offered, and his championing of the Vietnam War alienated younger audiences. Yet he prevailed, mostly because of the reservoir of goodwill he had stored up by entertaining the American military on all its battlefields, in all its wars, for a half-century. Those lonely young men, fac-ing death, wanted cheek and sass, a moment's escape, girl gags, second-lieutenant gags, K-ration gags—well-machined jokes that drowned out the machinery of war. They loved him for the trouble he took on their behalf. And so did we. ∎

THE LOOK: Hepburn in 1942. Though she was beautiful, the young Kate was far too ornery and untamable to become a standard Hollywood starlet

1907-2003

A Yankee Schoolmarm in Hollywood's Court

Star, icon, fighter, lover: Katharine Hepburn taught women to walk tall

FILM STARS TYPICALLY POSSESS A GLAMOROUS VERSION OF the common touch; they are of the earth. Katharine Hepburn was apart and above, an aristocrat from some loftier time. But she was no standard Great Lady; her emotional intelligence was too prickly. She blew hot and cold in the same breath—her fire had Freon in it. For 60 years, moviegoers couldn't keep their eyes off her. She was often parodied but never duplicated. A promising new actress might be

called a Marilyn Monroe type or a Meryl Streep type, but there was no Kate Hepburn type. There was only Kate Hepburn. With her death at 96, cinema lost its domineering goddess.

That flinty spirit was born and bred in Hepburn. Her father, a surgeon, campaigned against venereal diseases. Her mother fought for legalized birth control and women's suffrage. "I was taught to speak out. My parents welcomed debate," Hepburn said in 1981. "My smell for reality comes from them." By rebelling, throughout her life, she was simply being a dutiful child.

She stormed Hollywood at 25 in the soaper *A Bill of Divorcement.* All elbows and eyes that raked the screen, Hepburn was immediately a star. Her studio, RKO, put her straight to work: 14 films in the next six years. A year after *Divorcement,* she played the headstrong, stagestruck ingenue in *Morning Glory* and won her first Oscar. The '30s were blessed with bright, beguiling actresses and superb roles tailored to their wit and independence. Hepburn got her share: the virginal "lady flyer" in *Christopher Strong,* the irresistibly manic Jo March in *Little Women,* the small-town social climber in *Alice Adams,* another terrific haughty-actress part in *Stage Door.*

She made her two best early comedies in 1938, both with Cary Grant: Philip Barry's rueful social comedy *Holiday,* then the frenzied farce *Bringing Up Baby,* in which she pours the anarchic energy of all the Marx Brothers into her slim, forceful form. She's jaw-droppingly enchanting in these two films, but by now her ferocious femininity had perhaps worn movie-

THE MEN: From left, with Jimmy Stewart in *The Philadelphia Story,* (1940); with Humphrey Bogart in *The African Queen* (1951); with Henry Fonda in *On Golden Pond* (1981), for which she won the last of her four Oscar awards

goers out. A prominent movie exhibitor declared she was "box-office poison," and just as quickly, RKO dropped her.

Not to worry: Hepburn had Barry write her a fat Broadway hit, *The Philadelphia Story.* She secured the movie rights, persuaded MGM to make it with her as the star and got pleasantly pawed by Grant and Jimmy Stewart. Hepburn was back to stay. But Barry's plot had given producers a naughty idea. If they couldn't tame Kate, they would put their annoyance with her airs in the script. From then on, many of her films—*Woman of the Year, The African Queen, The Rainmaker*—are about the coarsening or humanizing of Hepburn by some rough all-American Joe.

Fortunately for Hepburn, the first of these Joes was Spencer Tracy. In him she met her match and the love of her life. Their film teaming was a union of equals, each distinct and distinguished, blending without surrendering a jot of their tetchy personalities. After Tracy's death, she showed she was still a game gal, tackling audacious roles from Mary Tyrone in *Long Day's Journey into Night* to Hecuba in *The Trojan Women* and Coco Chanel on Broadway.

Nowadays actresses are told they are obsolete in their 30s or 40s. At twice those ages, Hepburn was too restless to retire, too smart to reduce her grandeur to sitcom size. After all, one must work, and standards must be maintained. There was a streak of the Yankee schoolmarm in her, and a tough grader at that. One imagines her reading her death notices—all raves—as if they were test papers. "Twaddle!" she would write in the margin. "You can do better. I did." And how. ∎

THE MAN: Hepburn never married Tracy, the one love of her life

1916-2003

The Real—and Reel—Gregory Peck

Onscreen and off, he showed that heroism can be humble

THE MOVIE STUDIO WANTED ROCK HUDSON TO PLAY ATTIcus Finch. Fate decreed otherwise. Gregory Peck got the role of the small-town Southern lawyer in the 1962 film version of *To Kill a Mockingbird*. The hero of Harper Lee's Pulitzer-prizewinning novel had been a man much like her father, and when the author met the actor on the first day of shooting, she noted, "Gregory, you've got a little potbelly just like my daddy." The star replied, "Harper, that's great acting."

Actually, it was great inhabiting. "You never really understand a person … " Atticus says, "until you climb inside of his skin and walk around in it." Tolerance ripening into empathy: that was Peck's gift in playing an elevated species of American, the man of strength and compassion. Today that species is more than endangered; it has nearly vanished. But it flourished during most of Peck's half-century in film, when Americans prided themselves on their fellow feeling for the downtrodden and their ability to uplift the races. Peck was liberal when liberal was cool.

From his early days as the most gorgeous man in pictures (in *Spellbound* and *Duel in the Sun*) to his long prime with a Mount Rushmore visage and the voice of Yahweh on a good day, Peck was the sonorous pitchman for movie humanism. He showed how a strong man could also be a gentle man. He counseled ethnic tolerance: of Jews, in *Gentleman's Agreement*, and blacks, in *Mockingbird*. As Finch, a crusading attorney who is also a gentle single dad to his two young kids, Peck made rectitude appear robust. That sanctity had staying power: in 2003 the American Film Institute chose Atticus Finch as the top hero in U.S. movie history.

Peck wasn't just an icon. He was an actor, a smart one. He picked hit properties in a wide variety of genres: romantic comedy (*Roman Holiday*), action (*The Guns of Navarone*), horror (*The Omen*). He was bold in taking roles—Ahab, General MacArthur—that twisted his noble-man image. He assayed his share of misanthropes (including Nazi monster

ALAN GRANT—TIME LIFE PICTURES

HANDSOME? You bet. But the star's real gift was to illuminate inner grace

Josef Mengele) and western hombres as craggy as a butte. But Peck will be best remembered as the movies' exemplary father figure, who often, and surprisingly, revealed the pacifism at the heart of heroism.

Good example: *Cape Fear*, with Peck as the head of a family menaced by all-time cunning sicko Robert Mitchum. At the climax, Peck trains a gun on the villain. Shoot 'im, Greg! But no. This time the good guy is not going to kill the bad guy; the rotter will be tried, convicted and imprisoned. A less confident actor might have let this verdict sound like weakness, but Peck sells the notion that life in jail is as unpleasant as a bullet in the gut.

Winners and losers are all too clearly defined in today's films. Peck's best movies always seemed to find thoughtful shades of gray. And while it's dangerous to confuse an actor with his movie roles, by all accounts the reel and the real Gregory Peck were close kin. He was a model of probity, a loyal friend to colleagues in distress, a father confessor to the Hollywood community. He chaired the National Society of This, the American Academy of That. He was laden with official honors; Lyndon Johnson gave him the Presidential Medal of Freedom; Richard Nixon put him on his enemies list. Peck received one of his sweetest laurels after he died, when the reclusive Lee, on hearing of his death, said, "Gregory Peck was a beautiful man. Atticus Finch gave him the opportunity to play himself."

But who will play the Gregory Peck hero now that noble is for wimps and the best place to find integrity is in *Webster's*? Peck's masculine delicacy is gone from films; no star has filled his shoes. Movie actors don't have the voice or posture or temperament for it. Maybe America can't believe in it. To cherish Peck is to admit nostalgia for an era when popular and political culture could champion humanist ideals without smirking. If our time were not so facetious, so often corrupt, that time—and this man—would not seem so precious. ◾

1932-2003

Three Chords and the Truth

In bone-deep songs, Johnny Cash bore witness to a lifetime of hard luck

FOR THE LAST 15 YEARS OF HIS LIFE, JOHNNY CASH'S MAIN job was to manage his almost constant pain. Decades of drug dependency, since conquered, had sapped him. So had heart surgery, diabetes and the medication he took for a misdiagnosed disease. Failing eyesight made it difficult for him to read his beloved books on Roman and early Christian history. A dentist, tending to Cash's teeth problems, had broken his jaw and never fixed it properly, the singer once said. Cash was then told he could have surgery, which might end his singing career, or take painkillers, which could retrigger his drug addiction. He chose instead to live with the pain—all of it. But then, his entire life seemed to be an exercise in controlling hurt, a dark journey by a man in black, illuminated only now and then by glimpses of blue sky overhead.

"I can't go on. I'll go on," wrote Samuel Beckett, whose plays and novels are no more depressing than your everyday country lament. John R. Cash had every right to sing the country blues. Demons found him even when he wasn't looking for them. He dressed like a hip coroner and sang like a gunman turned Pentecostal preacher. His haunting songs perfectly matched his haunted voice. Before Cash, rarely had a singer taken pain and made it so audible, so immediate, so dark and deep. Rarely had a voice also shown the grit to express, endure and outlive that misery. His songs played like confessions on a deathbed, delivered with the plangent stoicism of a jailbird.

Cash's music is not so much out of fashion as above it. His CDs are found in the country section of the music store, but he doesn't quite fit there. He came up with rockabilly phenoms like Elvis Presley and Jerry Lee Lewis, but few of his songs were hard-driving rave-ups. *I Walk the Line, Ring of Fire, Folsom Prison Blues*—these are, if anything, contemporary folk songs. Cash sang of specific injustices and eternal truths; he was the deadpan poet of cotton fields, truck stops and prisons.

OUT OF STYLE: Balladeer of darkness, Cash usually wore black to perform

He was a balladeer, a spellbinding storyteller, a witness, in the Christian sense of the word. Here was a man who knew the commandments because he had broken so many of them.

He was born into adversity, as the fourth of five children of farmers in Depression-wracked Kingsland, Ark., where cotton was the Cash crop. After high school, he worked at an auto plant in Michigan and served a hitch overseas with the Air Force. He came home, married Vivian Liberto and settled with her in Memphis, Tenn. This was in 1954, and by the next year he had a deal with Sun Records, which had launched Presley's career. He moved to Columbia records in 1958, and reached a peak of popularity and artistic energy in the early '60s, when his exhilarating, exhausting schedule of live performances led to drug and alcohol binges and the failure of his marriage. Cash saw the light in 1967, when he began spending quality time with June Carter of the legendary Virginia-mountain country clan the Carter family, who reintroduced him to his deep-rooted Christian faith; they married in 1968.

A solid marriage doesn't guarantee career longevity, but Johnny Cash managed both. He invited Bob Dylan to Music City to perform on his TV show. Later, Cash did guest turns on albums with Ray Charles, Emmylou Harris and U2. In the 1980s, he teamed up with Willie Nelson, Waylon Jennings and Kris Kristofferson for a sometime country supergroup, the Highwaymen. After one of his occasional career rough patches, Cash found a sympathetic producer in rock-and-rap pro Rick Rubin in 1994. In a series of four stunning albums, Rubin returned Cash to his roots: the voice, a guitar and the sparest backing. They weren't giant sellers, but they validated Cash's towering stature. His last video, a version of the song *Hurt*, by Trent Reznor of the band Nine Inch Nails, brought his life full circle. It is an intense cry of pain dished out, pain absorbed—and pain turned into art. For one last time, Cash was hurting, but in control. ∎

REUTERS NEWS MEDIA—CORBIS

Idi Amin
1925(?)-2003

During an eight-year reign that plunged a prosperous Uganda into desperate poverty, the onetime military boxing champ used slaughter as a form of statecraft. The son of a peasant farmer and a mother who practiced sorcery, the nearly illiterate Amin joined the British colonial army in 1946. Nine years after Uganda achieved independence in 1962, he led a successful coup, then embarked on murderous campaigns against political opponents and rival ethnic groups that left as many as 500,000 dead. He also expelled thousands of Asian traders, depriving Uganda of much of its business class. The ruthless dictator, who cultivated rumors he practiced cannibalism, was ousted at last in April 1979, after Tanzanian troops, responding to a Ugandan invasion, entered the capital of Kampala and forced him to flee. He found asylum in Saudi Arabia, where he lived a life of luxury with one of several wives and 22 of his children.

Daniel Patrick Moynihan
1927-2003

The great Senator was working-class New York City's most exquisite son, a book-hungry street genius with a fresh, vital intellect built from the pavement up. Raised by his mother, on and off the dole, he shined shoes after school near the New York Public Library. He was an inconvenient man who believed ethnicity was a more potent predictor of political behavior than social class. He outraged liberals by insisting that too many black kids were being raised without fathers; he outraged conservatives by opposing Bill Clinton's welfare reform because he didn't want to see those children hurt. He was an avid patriot and anticommunist, especially when he served as U.S. ambassador to the U.N. He drank like a fish, wrote like a dream and stood in the Senate like Cicero.

TERRY ASHE—TIME LIFE PICTURES—GETTY IMAGES

AP/WIDE WORLD

Strom Thurmond
1902-2003

The longest-serving U.S. Senator in history, South Carolina's Thurmond will be forever linked to his early, often hateful-sounding rhetoric opposing civil rights and racial integration. He made a failed bid for the White House in 1948 as nominee of the "Dixiecrat" states' rights parties and initiated the "Southern Manifesto," calling for resistance to the 1954 Supreme Court ruling that integrated public schools. Over the course of 48 years in the Senate, Thurmond adroitly shifted his views with the times. He was among the first Southern G.O.P. Senators to hire a black aide, he voted to extend the Voting Rights Act, and in 1983 he supported creating a federal holiday to honor Martin Luther King Jr.

Edward Teller
1908-2003

Born in Hungary, the brilliant physicist had a longer and more intimate acquaintance with nuclear weapons than any man in history. A rabid anticommunist, he pushed for development of the hydrogen bomb but was reviled by many of his peers for implying that his onetime boss, J. Robert Oppenheimer, was a national security risk. In the 1980s Teller backed Ronald Reagan's nukes-based Star Wars program.

Bill Mauldin
1921-2003

With Willie and Joe, the unshaven, hollow-eyed, grimy World War II dogfaces, Mauldin created an unlikely and imperishable pair of American icons. The duo first appeared in the pages of the Army newspaper *Stars and Stripes,* fighting not just the Germans during the Italian campaign but also tedium, wet socks, lousy K rations and their commanding officers. G.I.s everywhere laughed, nodding in rueful recognition. Mauldin combined the satiric eye and brush of a Daumier with the ear of a Ring Lardner. His war works won Mauldin a Pulitzer Prize in 1945, and the 23-year-old, who had grown up poor in the Southwest, found himself an uncomfortable celebrity. He became an editorial cartoonist and won his second Pulitzer for a cartoon in the St. Louis *Post-Dispatch* in 1959; he moved to the Chicago *Sun-Times* in 1962 and stayed there 30 years.

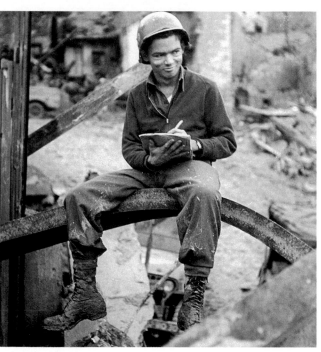

Madame Chiang Kai-shek
1897-2003

Charismatic, imperious and profoundly anticommunist, the wife of Chinese Nationalist leader Chiang Kai-shek was one of the world's most powerful women for decades. TIME named the couple Man and Woman of the Year 1937, as the two battled the Japanese invasion of Manchuria. At home with the silvery pleasantries of the social world and with the adamantine realities of the political, the woman born Soong Mei-ling won many supporters in the U.S., where she was educated. She remained a forceful voice in Chiang's government when the couple fled to Taiwan after Mao Zedong's victory over the Nationalist forces in 1949.

David Brinkley
1920-2003

The pioneering TV newsman's clipped, sardonic delivery made him one of the medium's most respected voices for four decades. Teamed with the more somber Chet Huntley, Brinkley enjoyed a 14-year-run on the NBC nightly news show, then was the host of a successful Sunday-morning talk show on ABC for 16 years.

Art Carney
1918-2003

His immortal turn as Ed Norton, the "underground sanitation expert" and upstairs neighbor to Jackie Gleason's Ralph Kramden on TV's *The Honeymooners*, was only a speck in a 50-year career that began in radio, flourished on Broadway and earned him an Oscar in 1974's *Harry and Tonto*. Carney as Norton proved that a second banana could be the top. A genius of body English, he walked in a springy slouch, his thin frame forming a question mark, his hands ever aflutter. Carney's Norton exuded a sweet assurance that life would treat him as he treated life: with an easy shrug and eager guffaw.

Sam Phillips
1923-2003

The prime impresario of rock 'n' roll didn't sing or play an instrument, but his ear was infallible. His Sun Records studio in Memphis, Tenn., was the home of raw genius, both black (Howlin' Wolf, B.B. King) and redneck (Carl Perkins, Johnny Cash, Roy Orbison). Phillips saw the huge potential in 18-year-old Elvis Presley in 1955 and produced the singer's finest early sessions.

John Ritter
1948-2003

The Emmy Award–winning actor and comedian energized the racy hit ABC sitcom *Three's Company* with his wit and slapstick moves. The son of country-and-western singer Tex Ritter, he worked frequently on TV and had roles in the 1996 film *Sling Blade* and on Broadway in Neil Simon's *The Dinner Party* in 2000. He died suddenly from a coronary-artery tear while taping his latest hit ABC sitcom, *8 Simple Rules*.

Leni Riefenstahl
1902-2003

The German filmmaker might have been remembered as cinema's greatest woman director or as its most gifted documentarian; her *Olympia*, a record of the 1936 Summer Games, pioneered techniques and attitudes copied in virtually all later TV sports coverage. Instead, she was vilified as the venal genius who glamorized the Hitler myth in 1935's *Triumph of the Will*, a record of a Nazi rally in Nuremberg. Riefenstahl outlived most of her critics but not her reputation; for 60 years she was blackballed from the medium she helped define.

Al Hirschfeld
1903-2003

He put motion and emotion in all his still lifes, bringing glamour and élan to a weighty Sunday paper. Over his 80-year career, Al Hirschfeld made hardly an in-apt stroke, and the comic muralist left behind a witty, insightful history of 20th century entertainers. Associated mainly with the New York *Times*, Hirschfeld drew—and drew out the spirit of—virtually every celebrity from high art to pop culture. Through his pen, inanity became animate, caricature met character, and readers became detectives—tracing his daughter Nina's name, cleverly hidden in his flowing lines. Above, he works on a 1999 cover for the TIME 100 series.

Fred Rogers
1928-2003

No, his first name wasn't Mister, but you can't blame generations of kids who grew up with Fred Rogers on TV for thinking that. The gentle kids' show host displayed an unabashed empathy for the emotional lives of children that made his Emmy-winning show, *Mister Rogers' Neighborhood*, TV's longest-running children's program. His leisurely style and pace created an island of tranquillity in the children's mediasphere of cartoons, robots and antic talking sponges. He was also unafraid to take on dark subjects: Rogers helped kids confront and understand divorce, death, shame, anger and fear. He spoke softly, but he never soft-pedaled, and he knew how to be both compassionate and authoritative.

Dolly the Sheep
1996-2003

The world's first cloned mammal was euthanized in Britain after being found to have a progressive lung disease. Created in 1996 with DNA taken from an adult ewe's cell, Dolly made headlines world-wide when she was born. But the sheep lived to only half the expectancy of her breed. Her early death and illnesses—she also had arthritis—raised serious questions about whether she had aged prematurely and about the safety of cloning.

Robert Atkins
1930-2003

The influential, hackle-raising weight-loss guru died of severe head injuries from a fall on an icy sidewalk in New York City. He first bucked convention in his 1972 best seller, *Dr. Atkins' Diet Revolution*, which advised dieters to trash the fruit salad in favor of high-protein, high-fat goodies like bacon cheeseburgers and butter, arguing that without carbohydrates to consume, the body would burn its own fat. Many of the 30 million who have tried the diet swear by it. But his regimen irritated mainstream medical groups, which called it extreme; the combative cardiologist breezily dismissed critics, saying, "My English sheepdog will figure out nutrition before the dietitians do." He never wavered from his conviction that his low-carb approach was the dieter's "magic breakthrough."

Dave DeBusschere

Charles Bronson, 81, roughhewn Hollywood B actor turned international movie hero. Born Charles Buchinsky, he was a solid ensemble player in films such as *The Dirty Dozen* and *The Great Escape* before starring as a vigilante who avenges the murder of his wife and rape of his daughter in the 1974 blockbuster *Death Wish.*

Herb Brooks, 66, coach in the most famous U.S. ice-hockey victory, the "Miracle on Ice," at the 1980 Lake Placid, N.Y., Winter Olympics.

Nell Carter, 54, multitalented, ebullient singer-actress who played the housekeeper in the 1980s sitcom *Gimme a Break!* and won a Tony in 1978 in the Broadway musical *Ain't Misbehavin'.*

Franco Corelli, 82, powerhouse Italian tenor. Largely self-taught, he was faulted by critics for the raw passion in his singing but adored by rank-and-file opera buffs.

Hume Cronyn, 91, wiry, perfectionist actor who infused his ordinary, usually cranky characters with bubbling intensity. He often appeared with his wife of 52 years, Jessica Tandy, who died in 1994; to her queen, he was the wry, uncommon commoner.

Dave Debusschere, 62, power forward who starred on the New York Knicks' championship teams of the early 1970s. The gritty defender and rebounder helped make those Knicks the smartest, most unselfish team in basketball history.

Larry Doby, 79, Hall of Fame slugger who became the first African American in the American League—just 11 weeks after Jackie Robinson broke the color barrier by joining the National League's Brooklyn Dodgers.

Buddy Ebsen, 95, gangly dancer turned TV star who played Jed Clampett in *The Beverly Hillbillies* and then folksy private eye Barnaby Jones.

Gertrude Ederle, 98, first woman to swim the English Channel. Her 1926 crossing took 14 hr. 31 min.

John Geoghan, 68, former priest imprisoned in 2002 for sexual abuse. He was killed by a fellow inmate. Revelations of Geoghan's misdeeds—130 people sued him for molesting them as children, but he was protected by superiors for years—led to a nationwide scandal for the Catholic church.

Althea Gibson, 76, tennis trailblazer. As the first African American to compete in a Grand Slam, winning titles at Wimbledon and the U.S. Nationals, she cleared a path for Arthur Ashe and the Williams sisters.

Buddy Hackett, 78, frenetic, old-school stand-up comedian, whose short, pudgy build and clownishly contorted expressions were on view in clubs, on TV and in such films as *The Music Man, It's a Mad, Mad, Mad, Mad World* and Disney's *The Love Bug.*

Bobby Hatfield, 63, the tenor half of the "blue-eyed soul" duo the Righteous

Buddy Hackett

Lester Maddox

Brothers, who brought an emotional passion to their music that was previously the province of black singers.

Gregory Hines, 57, elegant modernizer of tap dance who showed his dazzling moves in film (*White Nights*), on TV and as a Tony-winning Broadway headliner (*Jelly's Last Jam*).

Maynard Jackson Jr., 65, who was elected Atlanta's first black mayor in 1973. He battled white business leaders to create economic opportunities for blacks and transformed Atlanta into a vital, progressive national hub.

Elia Kazan, 94, actor and film and stage director. He made socially conscious films that challenged U.S. social attitudes, while directing stars like Marlon Brando, who brought a new proletarian vitality to stage and screen.

Michael Kelly, 46, gifted journalist and editor (*Atlantic Monthly*). He was killed on assignment in Iraq in a humvee accident while traveling as an "embedded" reporter with the U.S. Army's 3rd Infantry Division.

Russell B. Long, 84, Democratic Senator from Louisiana for 38 years. He was responsible for the earned-income tax credit and the $1 taxpayer checkoff box to fund presidential campaigns.

Lester Maddox, 87, flamboyant restaurant owner turned segregationist Georgia Governor. He gained local notoriety by loudly refusing to serve three black Georgia Tech students in his

Pickrick Restaurant in the wake of the newly signed Civil Rights Act.

Donald O'Connor, 78, rubber-limbed actor-dancer who brought an irrepressible vaudeville energy to films and TV. In the *Make 'em Laugh* number in *Singin' in the Rain,* he created the greatest comic dance solo in film history.

Adam Osborne, 64, executive who in 1981 introduced the first portable PC. With its 5-in. screen, the 24-lb. Osborne 1 elicited a frenzy of orders before manufacturing glitches derailed it.

Robert Palmer, 54, natty Brit-rock eminence of the '80s. In his sexy videos, leggy ladies struck poses while a fuzzy

George Plimpton

bass line growled under Palmer's knowing vocals. His self-bestowed title: the James Bond of boogie.

Suzy Parker, 69, 1950s supermodel whose red hair, green eyes and much envied bone structure made her Coco Chanel's "signature" face and the highest-paid model of her day.

George Plimpton, 76, man of letters who, as editor of the *Paris Review,* championed promising writers. As a participatory journalist, he pitched to Willie Mays and tried out for the Detroit Lions. Plimpton guest-starred on *The Simpsons,* danced at Truman Capote's Black and White Ball and witnessed the assassination of Robert Kennedy. Though he loved to play the underdog's role, he never lost his dignity or his wry, twinkly-eyed patrician charm.

Donald Regan, 84, former head of Merrill Lynch who left to become Ronald Reagan's Treasury Secretary and then chief of staff, where he ran into trouble: the Iran-*contra* scandal blew up on his watch, and he tangled with the First Lady, who helped speed his ouster after a year.

Herb Ritts, 50, easygoing celebrity photographer whose ability to make famous subjects comfortable helped him capture and define the glamour and narcissism of the 1980s.

Walt Rostow, 86, good-natured yet hawkish adviser to Presidents Kennedy and Johnson whose unfailing optimism about U.S. involvement in Vietnam helped propel the war.

Edward Said, 67, Columbia University scholar, author of the influential study *Orientalism* and the most prominent advocate for Palestinian independence in the U.S.

Nina Simone, 70, fiery singer and classically trained pianist who appealed to fans for her alternately smooth and gravelly tones, majestic stage presence and maverick opinions.

Walter Sisulu, 90, steadfast, low-profile crusader against apartheid who, with close friend Nelson Mandela, led the African National Congress (A.N.C.) and engineered the struggle for South African democracy.

Warren Spahn, 82, Hall of Fame pitcher who won 363 games, more than any other left-hander in major league history. He and Boston Braves teammate Johnny Sain inspired the motto of hopeful Braves fans during the 1948 World Series: "Spahn and Sain, and pray for rain."

William Steig, 95, humanely perceptive cartoonist and illustrator for the *New Yorker* for seven decades who, at age 60, began a successful second career writing children's books, including *Shrek,* a tale of a green ogre.

Joe Strummer, 50, punk rock's godfather. His seminal band the Clash drove punk to adventurous heights, taking

Walter Sisulu

political stances and urging action against social injustice and pretentious poseurs.

Sir Wilfred Thesiger, 93, indefatigable British explorer and travel writer and the first Westerner to twice cross Saudi Arabia's vast, uncharted Empty Quarter. His credo: "The harder the life, the finer the person."

Barry White, 58, R.-and-B. singer and disco love god whose distinctive voice, a deep, elegant and irresistible bass baritone, was legendary for its romantic, mood-altering powers. Hip-hop artists still turn to his work when they need a sexy, sultry sample.

Warren Zevon, 56, morbidly witty rock-'n'-roll poet and reformed drinker whose musical tales (*Werewolves of London, Excitable Boy*) included tender ballads, true-crime tales and bluesy odes to doom and death.

Barry White